The Legend of
Thunder Canyon

The True Story of an Epic Deer Hunt

in Michigan's Upper Peninsula

DUANE PAPE

DEDICATION

Part I of this book is dedicated to all the big bucks in the big woods who live their lives every day in the places we would rather be.

***

Part II of the book is dedicated to all the deer hunters young and old, who tried and failed in the moment of truth, then dared to dream of redemption.

***

And for all the hunters who hunt for more than the kill: May you find happiness in the woods and fields long after your killing days are done.

CONTENTS

CONTENTS

AUTHOR'S NOTE

I swear to tell the truth, the whole truth,
and nothing but the truth.

Sometimes storytellers will bend the truth as they weave their yarns.

Fishermen, in particular, have at times earned dubious reputations
by stretching the truth and creating whoppers.

Even hunters have been known to tell tall tales on occasion.

What I'm here to tell you is a story composed entirely of the
complete straight truth. The characters described herein are real
people using their real names.

The only variance from fact can be found in the place names.
In order to protect the secrecy of my spots, I have slightly
adjusted the real names of my favorite places.

While my adventures have at times seemed unbelievable even to me,
the stories I share in this book are 100 percent true.
No embellishment, no exaggeration, no bull.

I hope you enjoy reading the stories as much as I enjoyed
experiencing the moments.

ACKNOWLEDGMENTS

As with most meaningful projects, this undertaking would not have been possible without the thoughtful contributions of the team.

First and foremost, I have to thank my lovely and patient wife. Thank you, Dawn, for your consistent and unwavering belief in me. Without your contributions, this project would never have been possible. Words cannot express my gratitude. Your love is the light in my life.

Second, I thank my thoughtful and supportive parents. Not only did they introduce me to the outdoors, but they also provided many great books which inspired me to create one of my own. Encouraging and patient, they were always helpful but never tried to steer my ship. Thank you.

Third, I give thanks to my friends and family for sharing in many of the adventures that have shaped my life. Thanks for spending your time with me in the great outdoors. And thanks for the memories.

Next, I offer my sincerest thanks to my closest confidants who took the time to review my writings and offer their sage advice as this project was under construction. Your sharp eyes and honest suggestions were integral to the development of the finished product.

Finally, I thank all the Yooper hunters mentioned in this book for simply being good guys and good sportsmen, and thanks to Old Joe for sharing the trail-cam photos of The Legend.

THE LEGEND OF THUNDER CANYON

Part I

1 THE HUNT OF A LIFETIME

Though I had never actually seen him, I knew he was out there. The buck of every deer hunter's dreams. The buck of a lifetime. I'd already been after him for two years prior to the 2015 deer season. In actuality, I'd been after him for more than two decades, paying dues with the hope of someday getting my chance at a giant whitetail buck in the big woods of Michigan's Upper Peninsula.

It's hard to tell exactly where this quest begins. For a lifelong deer hunter, it seems one story leads into the next, and they all become one, the story of a hunter's career. As for my story, since 1986 I had sought to prove I was more than a flash in the deer hunting pan.

In the nearly thirty years since '86, I had harvested many respectable bucks in Michigan, but never anything close to the massive eleven-pointer I managed to tag in my second year of deer hunting.

We called the big guy Mr. B.G. In the spring and summer of that year, we had seen him several times on our farm in southern Michigan. It was the kind of deer that would induce a case of buck fever in anyone, any time of the year. He was a 240-pound monster of a buck and took honors as the largest eleven-point and the biggest buck harvested by a youth in Michigan that season. And like any foolish and ambitious young fella might do, I went ahead and told people I planned to get a bigger one the next year.

Silly boy.

Nearly three decades later, I had yet to make good on that boyhood plan. Oh, I had a couple chances at monster bucks as a young man while I still lived in farm country, but those opportunities ended in abject failure. Failure that I still recall all too vividly. You never forget the stories of the times you blew it.

The author (right) with "Mr. B.G." at the 1987 Michigan Deer Spectacular. The deer was the largest eleven-pointer taken in the state during the 1986 season.

I suppose I could've been satisfied in having already taken my buck of a lifetime, but that was nearly a lifetime ago. Besides, hunting deer in the farmlands of southern Michigan is a vastly different game than hunting big bucks in the big woods up north. As a young fella, I'd reached the pinnacle of success in farmland deer hunting.

As a man, the one thing I had left to do in my hunting career was to hunt down the buck of a lifetime in the big woods. After more than twenty years of hunting in the U.P. and not getting a single chance at a true monster buck, I was beginning to think my lack of luck might be some sort of jinx.

Jinxed or not, my story of deer hunting has evolved into a full-fledged quest for an almost mythical beast, like seeking a creature as rare as a three-horned unicorn. It's become a lifelong pursuit, an all-encompassing saga of a hunt now spanning thirty years. It's the quest to participate in the hunt of a lifetime and to hunt the buck of a lifetime.

Through the course of more than thirty years of deer hunting, I've found that my goals have shifted. In the early years, the goal was simply to get a buck. With a family of five, we depended upon the food we could harvest ourselves. In those days, with limited time to hunt, the harvest of a buck of any size was one to be celebrated.

Some of the results after more than thirty years of hunting in Michigan.

These days, with a family of three and a diet comprised of more than eighty percent grains and vegetable matter, we're less dependent on wild game for survival. With more time available to dedicate to hunting, nowadays my goal in hunting is less to get a buck, and more to experience all that's associated with deer hunting. In other words, it's more about the quality of the overall experience than it is about killing an animal.

After more than three decades of dedicated hunting experience, I've come to possess hunting skills on an elite level. With my level of experience in hunting whitetails, it would be easy to go out most days and have a chance to harvest a little buck. Perhaps too easy for the modern me.

No longer am I hunting just for the meat. Likewise, no longer am I satisfied with the relative lack of challenge in trying to harvest a naive young buck. With all due respect to the little deer of this world, the fact is, with their limited experience, they're no longer a worthy adversary for me.

Anymore, I find myself to be more of a hunter of great adventure. Sure I'm hunting deer, but not just any little deer will do. I'm looking for something special. More than to kill an animal, I'm seeking to be the best hunter that I can be. And the best way I can reach the pinnacle of success as a deer hunter is to face off against an equal adversary on a neutral playing field.

What I now seek is a shot at the title belt against the undisputed champ, a chance to step in the ring and do battle with the King of the Mountain.

Any fisherman can go and catch a little minnow. I want more. Like a fisherman with a lifetime of experience, I want to finally land the lunker of a lifetime, the fish of 10,000 casts.

Being a seasoned athlete at the top of my game and at the peak of my career, I hope to achieve the highest accomplishment in my chosen sport. Like a pro golfer who wants to win the Masters, a sprinter who hopes to win the Olympic gold, or a ballplayer wanting to win a world championship, my desire is to be the best at what I do.

It's not about the size of the trophy, the gold in the medal, nor is it for the fame or fortune. It's about pouring all my effort, all that I've learned, all my physical skill and will, into achieving the goal of being the best I can possibly be.

My intent is to earn that proverbial green jacket, and not for the warmth or style of wearing it. Rather, I want it for all it represents. Because to wear the green jacket, you have to be the best. And to be the best, you have to perform nearly flawlessly, endure whatever adversity you face, and have the strength, will, and endurance to fight to the end.

More than anything, I want to taste the satisfaction of achieving a most difficult goal for which I've strived for so long. I'm ready to tackle the most difficult challenges and prepared to face the toughest opponent head on.

And this time, I intend to win.

2 BIG WOODS, BIG BUCKS, BIG CHALLENGES

Hunting deer in the big woods of Michigan's Upper Peninsula can be one of the most challenging hunts of all. Deer there are relatively rare, terrain is tough, and deer activity is, more often than not, predictably unpredictable. While hunters in southern Michigan's farm country often see twenty or more deer and multiple bucks in a single day, hunters in the U.P. may not see twenty deer or multiple bucks during an entire season.

Although the number of deer in the big woods pales in comparison to farmland populations, hunting the north woods holds one advantage over the farmlands. In the big woods, the country is big, the hunting pressure is minimal, and the result is that many bucks survive from season to season to eventually reach full maturity.

Four-, five-, and six-year-old bucks are present in the population every year. Though actual sightings of these reclusive beasts are rare, each year they leave their sign in the hills, and each year someone in the area tags a true monster buck. Those big old bucks are wary, wise, exceptionally strong, and possess all the knowledge of the hills. As they grow old in their rough terrain, they seemingly become unkillable. With so many advantages in their favor, it's not unusual for big woods bucks to die of old age.

To actually work your way into an opportunity at a gigantic old buck in the big woods is one of the most difficult challenges in all of the hunting world. Doing it the old-fashioned way, without a blind, without bait, on the ground, on the buck's turf and on his terms, well, that's stuff for the top shelf, right next to the impossible.

While difficult, hunting deer in the big woods of the U.P. is definitely not impossible. In fact, with significant effort, many skilled hunters in the U.P. regularly harvest nice bucks in the two- and three-year-old age class. With a lot of persistence and a little luck, a few hunters eventually get chances at one of those elderly and elusive monster bucks.

Hunting in the big woods of the Lake Superior basin is often a big challenge. Most years, you're likely to see more big snow than big bucks.

Many times, the story of a hunter tagging a lifetime buck is one of dumb luck. Like the guy who parks the truck, walks a few steps up the hill, and minutes later a huge buck comes trotting down the hill chasing a doe. Or the guy who drives around all day road hunting, sees a huge buck, hops out, and shoots the deer while it stands there and watches. Or the young kid (ahem) who stumbles into getting one of the biggest bucks ever in only his second year of hunting. Or the hunter in the middle of answering the call of nature, and here comes ...

Not me. If I was ever going to get another buck of a lifetime, I was determined to earn it. No dumb luck here. I planned to take the battle to the opponent, on his turf and his terms, hoping that through hard work, I could overcome all the obstacles in the way.

I was determined to find success at the most difficult task in all of deer hunting: to harvest a mature buck in the big woods without the use of a blind or bait. I wanted to do it the old-fashioned way or not at all. Win or lose, I wanted a fair challenge on a level playing field. More than that, I wanted to get in the ring and take my best shot at the King of the Mountain. Although I had lofty aspirations, I felt ready to do whatever was necessary to get the job done.

3 A SEED IS PLANTED

In late November 2013, I returned to the place I call Fifteen-Point Mountain, in search of the buck that had thoroughly broken the rack of the three-year-old eight-point that I'd harvested earlier that season. With a few inches of fresh sloppy snow on the ground, I was hoping to find a big buck track to follow.

Having spent more than twenty years hunting in the big woods and deep snows of the Upper Peninsula, I've found one of the most effective ways to hunt big bucks is to simply follow their tracks in the snow. It's also my favorite style of hunting. Under the perfect conditions and in the right situations, it can be surprisingly easy to sneak right up close to unsuspecting deer. Now I use the terms simply and easy relatively loosely here. Because the fact is, trying to get a buck by following his tracks in the snow is usually the most difficult of all types of deer hunting. But it's also one of the best ways to consistently get chances at big bucks. It's hard work, but if you work hard enough, eventually it'll be worth the effort. Because every once in a while, after working your tail off for many days, suddenly everything comes together, and all of a sudden, there he is right in front of you. In that moment, it can seem so easy … until you consider all it took to arrive at that moment.

Win or lose, tracking is probably the most exciting form of deer hunting. It's also the best way to learn about deer behaviors, territories and movement patterns in the areas you hunt. And once in a while, when everything comes together, it seems to be the perfect way to hunt.

Looping around the south side of the mountain, I found his tracks in the snow, heading uphill. It was the kind of track that stops you in your tracks. With huge feet and a long and wide-spaced stride, it was undoubtedly the

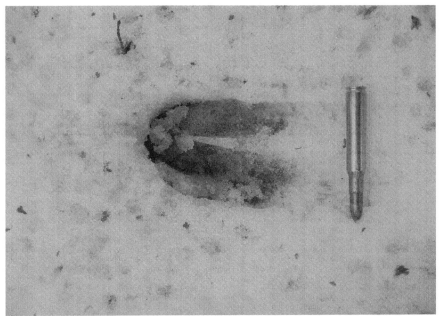

When you see a track as wide as a .30-06 cartridge is long, it was likely left by a big buck.

spoor of a super-buck. Unlike anything else in the area, anything I had seen for years in fact, it looked like a cow track among goat tracks. As I studied the footprints in the snow, I tried to imagine what the deer might look like. No doubt made by a 250-pound animal, I knew I was looking at the track of a true buck of a lifetime.

While it was a little late in the day to make a start, at 3 p.m. I followed the tracks up the hill. Making his way up the mountain, the buck checked in with all the spots where does had recently been feeding.

Slowly sneaking and peeking my way up the hill, excitement oozing from my pores, I carefully made my way along his trail. Although the wind was not exactly perfect, I continued after him.

Cresting the hill, his tracks looped around, then eventually worked down to a ledge on the east side of the peak. Sneaking down and around the side of the hill with the wind at my back, I found his fresh bed from which he had recently and hastily vacated. He had winded me and headed down to the east.

By this time, the clock had rolled to 4 p.m. and I figured it was time to let him go for the day. The last thing I wanted to do was chase him out of the area. Reluctantly, I turned and left the track and headed for the truck.

Little did I know, this track would lead to a story spanning several years. And while I continued to look for his track for the remainder of 2013, our paths would never cross again that season.

2014: The Season Without a Season

Thinking about that super-buck whose tracks I'd located in 2013, I was eager to start the 2014 season. On November 10, while scouting an area near where I'd found that huge track the previous year, I was lucky enough to find a shed antler from a nice eight-pointer, dropped the previous winter. I had always suspected that big bucks used the area, and now I had some tangible proof.

Better yet, the whole area was littered with scrapes and rubs. Just a few more days, I thought, and I'll be back on his track. The weather forecast called for a snowstorm, so I was confident I would soon find a good track to follow.

Then came the blizzard of 2014. On November 11, the snow began, and snow it did for three straight days. By the time November 15 arrived, we had a solid thirty-three inches of new snow on the ground. And the 2014 season was over before it started. All the side roads and bush trails were completely impassable to truck traffic. Only snowmobiles, trail groomers, or bulldozers were going anywhere. Thousands of U.P. hunters were shut out, unable to even get to camp.

Not only was it a disaster of a deer season for nearly all the hunters, but for the deer who had survived the previous coldest winter ever, this was a double shot of doom, with impossible amounts of snow and record cold. The conditions buried all of the food on the ground. Forced to move early to already depleted winter yarding areas, the struggling deer herd faced another challenging winter right from the get-go.

A nice shed antler found less than a week before the 2014 Opening Day.

Heavy snow in mid-November 2014 made woods travel nearly impossible.

Needless to say, I never got a chance to go anywhere near the home range of the super-buck in 2014 and never got to see his giant track. And while I did get to hunt that season in the lower elevations, I saw few deer and got only one opportunity at a small buck. (That's a story for another day.)

For the deer, 2014 was a much-needed reprieve from the pressure of hunters. Most hunters never made it to the woods, and those who did found the going to be extremely difficult. With hunter participation and success at an all-time low, most of the adult bucks survived the season.

4 THE QUEST CONTINUES

Keeping an eye on the weather forecasts heading into the 2015 season, it was becoming clear that this year was going to be much different from the previous year. The weather was shaping up to be the exact opposite of 2014's blizzard season, with long-range forecasts calling for temps in the 40s and 50s and absolutely no snow on the horizon. If nothing else, at least the weather looked like it would allow for good travel conditions in the big woods.

Meanwhile, forecasts from the biologists were calling for unprecedented lows in deer populations and a significant lack of young bucks in the herd. On the bright side, DNR officials predicted there would be more mature bucks in the woods for 2015, with a larger proportion of the harvest expected to be comprised of three- and four-year-old bucks.

My excitement for the season was compounded by the fact that during the summer and early fall, I'd seen more big bucks in my travels than ever before.

Along with the buck sightings, I was looking forward to using the fancy new scope I mounted on my rifle. In fact, the day I went to sight-in the new scope, I saw a huge buck in the middle of the day, right in the core of my favorite new hunting area. Needless to say, I was stoked.

Having learned so much in previous years and having upgraded my equipment to the best possible setup, I was convinced that I was now prepared to be a better hunter than ever before. Combine that with my superior physical shape after training for two years on the daily two-mile mountain hikes with my pound-hound, and I was more than ready to go.

While I normally like a little snow for the hunting season, I was reminded in 2014 that too much of a good thing can be a bad thing. After the arctic weather we faced the previous year, I was looking forward to stretching my legs and venturing deep into the unknown on bare ground.

The outlook for 2015 called for mild weather and more big bucks than usual.

After finding some new territory in the previous few years, I was eager to expand my explorations to connect all the new places I'd seen in the huge map of my mind. In particular, I was eager to explore a couple mountain ranges isolated from the beaten path by rivers, rough terrain and a lack of roads.

Knowing there would be more big bucks in the woods this year than in most years and thinking I might be on to some new places with great potential, I had a feeling this might be a special year. I didn't know exactly where I'd find what I'd been looking for, but I knew I was getting closer to the proverbial pot of gold.

Somewhere out there, the buck of my dreams was living comfortably, well on his way to dying of old age. I knew he was out there, and this year I was bound and determined to find him. While it looked like I might not have snow for tracking, what I would have is the ability to venture far and wide without being bogged down by ridiculous amounts of snow as I looked for his sign.

Sooner or later, if nothing else, the law of averages would have to lead me to that once-in-a-lifetime opportunity. It seemed that my lucky number would have to be called eventually. And after thirty years of paying dues, I had a feeling that perhaps my moment was about to arrive.

5 WHERE TO GO AND WHY

Deep in the heart of the central Upper Peninsula, the area I hunt is an expanse of some of the wildest woods east of the Mississippi River. Often referred to as the Huron Mountains or the Michigamme Uplands, this block of wilderness is comprised of hundreds of square miles of the most rugged and remote lands that Michigan has to offer. Spanning the north-central Upper Peninsula in the counties of Baraga and Marquette, my hunting grounds are so extensive, I could never hunt every acre of possibility in ten lifetimes. It's a wild-man's wonderland with few roads, even fewer people, and hundreds of square miles of uninhabited wilderness.

With multiple bedrock mountains in the area rising up to nearly 2,000 feet, the area is steep, rocky, and rough. Interspersed among these hills and canyons are pockets of prime deer habitat featuring large stands of mature oaks, dense stands of balsam and pine thicket, and vast expanses of open hardwoods. At the bottoms of the hills and canyons, dense tag alder strip-swamps meet expansive swamps choked with alder, balsam, cedar, black spruce, and willow.

Cutting through the core of this ancient mountain range, many wild and scenic rivers and creeks snake their way through the rugged and vast expanse of deep woods. Flowing generally to the east and north, the rivers are joined by dozens of smaller creeks and trickles as the flows cascade hundreds of feet downhill, tumbling over multiple waterfalls in the perpetual journey to Lake Superior. Thundering through canyons and around bends, the rivers make many unnamed drops before plummeting over more renowned falls. Near the respective headwaters of these wild and scenic rivers are vast roadless tracts, comprised of tens of thousands of acres of public lands.

It's in these upper elevations of the Lake Superior watershed that I base my adventures, where the hills are high, the canyons are deep, and the lands

One of the many canyons found in the mountains of the Upper Peninsula.

between are jagged and steep. It's a land where few men dare to go. Finding the time to hunt in such a remote spot is the first challenge. The bigger challenge is finding the strength and the will to walk these hills day after day. It's big country, and the huge challenge of hunting there is part of what draws me back every year.

Now, after twenty years of boldly going and exploring my hunting area, I've found that my traditional hunting range is shrinking somewhat. With extensive scouting logged into my database, I've begun to recognize patterns of deer activity that have led me to focus on some specific key areas. For many years I had searched far and wide for the perfect hunting area. In those years, I'd logged hundred of miles in the truck, looking for buck tracks to take, then following those bucks through their range. While I'd found some good spots along the way to harvesting many decent bucks, I also found there are many areas where the hunt for a deer would be akin to a hunt for a McDonald's on the moon.

For 2015, I planned to focus most of my effort toward a single area, a diverse and rugged section I now call the Nine-Mile Square. It was an area I discovered in 2012. In that season, I began to narrow my search for the best hunting area after changes in many previous hot-spots had led to more people traffic in those areas. Looking for the perfect spot, I needed tough terrain with limited access, good deer populations with slim human populations, and I wanted some steep and deep country that wasn't too big to hike. Above all, I wanted to hunt an area with the potential to produce a buck of a lifetime.

15

The Nine-Mile Square was an area I had stumbled into a couple of times over the years while exploring in the off-season. Whenever I went there, I always saw impressive buck sign. On my first hunt in the area in 2012, I snuck up on a nice buck who was napping under some hemlocks. Subsequent trips there in '12 yielded many more buck sightings. Then in mid-December of that season, I was able to sneak up on a nice buck bedded on a mountain. That deer turned out to be the first buck I ever harvested with my muzzleloader. It was an area big enough to spend several years exploring, and all indications pointed to this place being *the* spot.

Why Go There?

Many hunters no longer hunt here. It's not like it used to be. There's fewer deer, more wolves, and the big bucks are nearly as rare as unicorns. With the big snows that the northern U.P. gets hammered with each year combined with an ever-expanding wolf population, the deer populations around here just can't seem to catch up with those in other places.

Certainly there is better deer hunting elsewhere, and many local hunters now do their hunting in Canada, Lower Michigan, Wisconsin, and other Midwest hunting hot-spots.

I suppose if I lived elsewhere I might not choose the immense challenge of hunting deer around here. But this is where I am. So I choose to make the best of my local opportunities. Sure, the odds of killing a big buck are extremely low. Sure, if I was just looking for food, I'd have better luck at the grocery store. But, for me, it's not about that.

Finding artifacts like this old saw adds to the fun of hunting in no-man's land.

An unexpected treasure discovered in 2010 while deer hunting in the wild U.P.

At this point in my career, it's not so much about how many deer I can see during the deer season. These days, it's more about the quality of the experience and finding the purest hunting adventure possible. It's about going into wild places, living like a wild-man, seeking and exploring, and discovering the natural happenings that go on every day in those natural places where few men have dared to venture. It's about connecting with nature and getting back to my natural roots as a creature, stripping away the technology which pervades our modern lives, and reverting to a simpler way of life. It's about living for a few weeks in a lifestyle more similar to that of my ancestors who roamed the earth for millennia before the advent of modern society. And when I'm out there, it's all about living in harmony with the natural world.

Of course, when deer hunting, the top priority is hunting deer, and for me, that's hunting for big, old bucks. But as any seasoned Upper Peninsula deer hunter knows, most moments of deer hunting do not include the actual shooting of a deer. In my estimation, the quality of my hunting experience can best be measured in all of those moments between the actual moments of the kill.

For me, a quality hunting experience can include seeing wolves, moose, bears, fishers, weasels, otters, owls, eagles, squirrels, or sometimes even a deer. Finding shed-antlers, artifacts, old railroad grades, ancient camp sites, new mountain views, unknown waterfalls, or sometimes an amazing line of rubs and scrapes, these are the things I live for in the hunting season.

An eye-to-eye meeting with this gigantic bull was the highlight of my 1999 deer season.

It's about heading out into the unknown each day and seeking the daily treasure, completely uncertain of what gift I might receive that day. In reality, actually getting a deer is as rare as fitting the last piece of the puzzle into place.

On good days, I'll see a few deer. Other times, I'll go several days between deer sightings. But deep down, I know there's always a chance I could cross paths with a buck of a lifetime in the big woods of the Upper Peninsula.

In these parts, the chances of seeing a big buck are nearly as good on the last day as the first. Because the terrain is so tough, the weather so wicked, and the population so sparse, the wild U.P. is one of the few places in the Midwest where a whitetail buck has a reasonable chance of dying of old age.

At times, completing the hunt can seem like an overwhelming puzzle as you can often go for days without putting a single piece in place. Other times, you stumble into the midst of a miracle, and all the pieces magically come together.

While those magical moments can be few and far between, in these deep woods, each day is an adventure, full of possibility and ripe with opportunity to go where seemingly no man has gone before. Perhaps that's the best thing about hunting the big woods. Most of the time, you feel like you've got the world all to yourself.

6 SEASON IN DEPTH

Originally, my intent in writing this story was to share the details of my hunting season with my far-flung hunting partners. It was a story too vast to share in the space of several phone conversations, so I figured the best way to share would be in a way that people could digest at their own leisure. In the end, I wanted for my partners to get a glimpse of my experience, to have the opportunity to join me and to share in the thrill of the hunt that I had worked so hard to find.

In order to get a true idea of the depth of the ongoing challenge I faced, I decided to share a little bit of each day afield during the course of this odyssey. Fortunately for the purpose of this project, I've carried a small notebook while hunting for the past several years. Dutifully, I've made the time to record my observations and findings each day, jotting down my thoughts and feelings as the season progressed. Decorated with sketches of woods scenes and plans for new inventions, this tattered and scribbled book of field notes serves as the framework and statistical basis for this story. (Later in the book, you'll see excerpts from that field journal and you'll notice they appear *in a different font*.)

Of course, some days result in more action than others. In fact, some days are downright boring. However, it's important to weigh all the results together in order to gain the adequate perspective to appreciate the magnitude of the challenge at hand.

This in mind, I hope you'll bear with me through the complete telling of the story, with apologies if it takes too long. At this point, I'm not sure just how many pages the story may consume, nor how long it will take to tell. I'm not even sure if the story is over yet. No matter. The first part of the story is already created in the history of time and space. My job is to tell that story, for better or worse.

Believe it or not, this is the true story of my 2015 hunting season.

November 15

Opening day 2015 began for me as many had in the previous decade, sitting under that old hemlock near Secret Lake, where Wolf Creek meanders between the three small oak-studded mountains.

At just before 9 a.m. I saw the movement of a critter coming my way. That's a ... a ... a wolf! A great big wolf at that. Like, as in, better than 100 pounds of carnivore big. Trotting in the golden light of morning, he passed by forty yards to the south of me, unaware of my presence, then headed west. Seconds behind him, there came another slightly smaller one, following the same path. Meeting up about sixty yards west of me, the wolves huddled together for a moment, then one headed southwest up the creek toward the beaver dam, while the other looped north, then west up and around the mountain.

With the exception of some squirrels and birds, those big dogs would prove to be all of the life I saw on opening day. Not exactly the opening day of deer season I had envisioned, but not a bad day either. No doubt it was a memorable day.

---Daily total: 0 deer, 0 bucks, 2 wolves

November 16

On the second day, I decided to head up into the hills where I found the shed antler in November 2014. I'd been thinking about the place for more than a year now and was prompt to arrive at the spot, with time to spare before daylight. After a half-mile hike in the dark, I settled in to a spot on the old logging trail where a ravine crossed. In front of me, a well worn deer trail emerged, then climbed the hill to the ridge overlooking the creek behind me.

As the sky revealed a hint of the day's first light, I heard the distinct sound of a deer's feet making a steady approach through the frosty leaves from the northwest. Still too dark for good visibility, I was hoping he would slow down and that daylight would hurry up and arrive. He paused a few times but not for long enough, and when he crossed thirty yards in front of me, it was still too dark to see. All I could make out was a vague silhouette, the dark shape of a large deer, moving through the woods the way I knew only bucks do. Bold, confident, early, sneaky, traveling alone, proceeding steadily and with a purpose. In my mind, I pictured a massive, gnarly old mossy-horn.

After he obliviously wandered past the silent sniper, the deer continued east until the sound of his steps faded away. Within a few minutes, the woods were illuminated with the morning's first light, and I strained to see some sign of the now departed deer. The oak plateau was interspersed with saplings, the result of a recent select cut, making visibility limited. Looking intently, I saw no sign of him.

Now mostly light, I knew the deer had to be near and I itched to try to find him. I thought, maybe if I sneak down the trail a bit, just maybe I can spot him.

Bad idea. I lifted my right foot to make that first step in his direction and: schnoort. Thoom, ta thoom, ta thoom, the big deer bounded down the ravine and away to the east. Turns out, he was within viewing range the whole time, watching me, and now he was long gone. Dammit. If I had only waited it out.

Later in the morning I climbed Lookout Mountain, a small, steep, 300-foot rock outcrop. Looking out over the valley below where two creeks converge, the view was tremendous. Though I saw only three deer on the day, I was excited to be hunting in this beautiful area.

---Daily total: 3 deer, 0 bucks. Season total: 3 deer, 0 bucks

November 17

Day three and once again, I was up and at 'em for first light. When I say up and at 'em, I mean out the door and on the road, well before first light. That means hearing the alarm at around 4 a.m., getting up, eating breakfast, tending to the daily bathroom duties, getting dressed, making lunch, and heading out the door just after 6 a.m. Then, day after day, it's on the road, through the bush to parts unknown, staying out in the woods from dawn until dusk. It's a daily routine that allows for little distraction and often amounts to little time for rest or sleep.

My plan this time was to make it a road hunt day. Rest the legs, check out where the deer are moving, where the other hunters are, and check in with all the spots that have produced results in years past. My route included a tour of most of the back roads in northern Marquette County and well into Baraga County. In traveling more than 100 miles in ten hours, I saw a total of five deer, all antlerless.

---Daily total: 5 deer, 0 bucks. Season total: 8 deer, 0 bucks

November 18

On day four I was unusually amped for the day ahead. My plan was to finally explore a mountain that, until this day, I could only scout via satellite photos and topographic maps. It was a place linked geographically to previous explorations and a place that looked to hold great promise. I couldn't wait to get my boots on the ground and scout this unique piece of geology. For more on that day's explorations, we'll refer to an excerpt from my field notes recorded that day.

November 18. South wind 20-35 mph, temperatures 53-56'.
6:20 - Leave camp.
6:50 - Arrive at the parking spot down by the creek.

7:10 - I settle into my sittin' spot. Extremely windy, gusts to 35 mph.
9:00 - No deer, not much moving except the slap happy beaver in the river at first light and the bald eagle who glided east on the wind. Too cold to sit around and wait. So I'm headed south to check some low country, then east up the mountain. It's a good day to explore new country. It's what I do.
10:00 - Arrive at west knob of mountain. Looks like rain.
12:00 - Approaching from the west, I follow the deer trail to the top of the mountain. The mountain is full of oaks, acorns, rubs, and scrapes. Big rubs. Good scrapes. Boy does this spot look good.
  Some old buck must have had a high time, rubbing most every tree on the way, making scrapes every 40-50 yards. I guess this place is his. The sign looks fresh, within the last week, but not today's. A few sprinkles and the wind is holding steady. Looks like a good place to hang around for a while.
2:30 - Lingering on the NW end of the mountain, hunkered under a couple balsams. The place is loaded with deer sign, littered with acorns, and decorated with perhaps the most and largest scrapes and rubs of any mountain-top that I have ever found. It's a fabulous spot. I WILL see a big buck here.
5:00 - Head out.
5:07 - One deer, spooked off west end of mountains, into lowlands.

One of many large scrapes found while exploring some new terrain.

A big rub along a line of dozens found on an oak-covered mountain.

As it turns out, this would be a pivotal day in my season. It was a day of discovery, when the treasure of where was presented to me. Unlike anything I'd ever seen, the mountain was decorated with at least forty scrapes and sixty rubs. It was the hunter's dream spot, the mountain of 100 signs. Now my job would shift. No longer did I need to seek the where. And I already knew the what and the who. Now I needed to find how to get myself into the precise moment when the right time and place converged, with me and the buck of a lifetime in the middle.
---Daily total: 1 deer, 0 bucks. Season total: 9 deer, 0 bucks

November 19
The fifth day of the season brought wind and rain, and yet again, I headed into the woods. This time, I headed out to explore the east slope of my new-found 100-Sign Mountain. Not every day yields immediate results and this was one of those days.

Actually, rain can be a nice thing for deer hunting. The moisture silences the crunch of the leaves underfoot, and the drips of the drops provide another layer of concealment, as the sounds of errant twigs breaking under foot merge with the sounds of the storm. In fact, with proper clothing, rainy days are some of my favorite days for hunting.

On this drizzly day, I was able to fill in some empty areas on my mental

map, and along the way I discovered yet more prime deer crossings. Though I was able to cover lots of ground quietly, I saw only one deer on the day. And that just so happened to be while I was taking a leak.
---Daily total: 1 deer, 0 bucks. Season total: 10 deer, 0 bucks

November 20

The sixth day brought a change in the weather. Conditions had gone from bad to worse. While the winds continued to howl as they had for the past four days, the mild air and mosquitoes had been replaced with wind chills and snow squalls. The blustery air with a wind chill around 15 degrees was a shock to the system. Worse, the previously soft forest under foot had been frozen and replaced with the equivalent of a carpet of potato chips, turning every careful step into an obnoxious cadence of crunch. Moving through the woods undetected on this day was hopeless. Not to mention, brrr!

Gentlemen, start your engines. Time to hit the road. Feeling a little weak, I decided it was good day to road hunt.

After patrolling some of my regular roads, I made my way to a favorite truck trail. Rounding the bend, headed down to the upper creek crossing, I saw him there in the road. It was my old friend Marv, who happened to be creeping up out of the creek in his venerable old Toyota. We met in the middle of the trail and shut down our rigs.

It was good to see an old friend, and old Marv is as good as it gets. Good people, he is. Though I only came to know him a few years ago, it's as if he's been a friend throughout the ages. Sort of like a friendly old mountain man that you meet while making your way through the mountains. Yeah, exactly like that. That's really how we met. Two mountain men making their way through the same mountain range.

Marv is a hunter cast from the same mold as myself. A tracker, stalker, supreme woodsman, and old fashioned deer hunter, he's like the Larry Benoit of the Upper Peninsula. Where I have plied my craft for two decades in the big woods of the U.P., Marv has spent the last five decades here honing his skills and regularly harvesting big bucks.

We are much alike. We hunt the same area, drive the same kind of truck, wear the same kind of wool clothes, and ironically, we both installed scopes on our guns for the first time this year. After years of success with iron sights, we both found our eyes were starting to go and finally decided the benefits of the new technology would outweigh the costs.

One of the things I like best about Marv, in conjunction with his encyclopedia of lively hunting stories, he is one straight shooter. Oh, I'm sure he's a good shot with his rifle too, but more importantly, he's straight up in his story telling. Not a bull-shitter, Marv tells it exactly like it is and even shares the details of where the story took place.

No exaggerations, no twisting the truth or being evasive with secret details, old Marv is an open book and shares those details that most other hunters would conceal. I suppose when you hunt the way we do, in the places we do, it doesn't really hurt to share the details. We know the vast majority of other hunters would never work up the determination to go where we go, let alone have the time to do so.

So we shared our stories and compared notes from last season. Not surprisingly, in the midst of the 2014 blizzard season, Marv took not one but two decent eight-point bucks.

As for this year, we were both still looking to see our first horns for the season. He then told me about the matched 8x7 moose sheds he recently found nearby, the big ten-pointer his brudder got on the first day this year, and he shared the stories of his recent deer hunt in Ontario.

As for the local scouting, he mentioned a mountain near the creek that was loaded with buck sign. He laughed as he described the amount of devastation the old buck had wreaked on that hill. Having scouted most of the mountains within a few miles, he said there was more sign on that one mountain than on all of the other hills combined.

I concurred. I wasn't planning on sharing my findings on that particular hill, but when Marv described the location and the sign to a tee, I admitted that I'd been similarly impressed when I walked the very same path.

It's a nice thing to share the stories and the scouting reports with a fellow hunter. To meet a stranger in the woods, become instant friends, and share the adventures like you would with a brother is a rarity in today's world. With the competitive and territorial nature of many of today's hunters, to find a friend like Old Marv is a gift not to be underestimated. We watched an eagle glide past, then wished each other well before we went our ways to continue our quests. Shortly after talking with Marv, I saw two deer just off the road, my only deer sightings on this cold and blustery day.

---Daily total: 2 deer, 0 bucks. Season total: 11 deer, 0 bucks

November 21

On the seventh day we finally got some decent hunting weather. With temperatures in the mid-20s and a few flurries in the air, I was excited for the day's hunt. With the woods too crunchy for a quiet approach, I cruised some two-tracks for the morning prime time, while in my mind I crafted my plan for the day. Knowing there were few places I could get into stealthily, I decided to go ahead and place stealth above all else.

The plan was to sneak along the creek and explore into the heart of a place I call Thunder Canyon. Figuring that the sound of the creek and waterfalls would cover the sounds of my steps, I set out for a pinch-point in the creek bottom, a sure-fire crossing for marauding bucks.

Easing down the stream, I took in the sights and sounds of the wild and flowing water. Along the way, I found several key deer crossings, along with a handful of prime trout hangouts. At the downstream end of the canyon, the stream makes a sharp turn just above the pinch-point. Creeping along the ancient creek-side trail, I made my way to the bend. At the narrows, I found a place to wait on a gravel bar at the stream's edge. It was a good spot that allowed visibility of up to 100 yards in several directions, a rarity amidst the tangled and densely wooded bottom land.

Tuning in to the Ishpeming High School football state playoff game on the radio, I stood for the national anthem, then settled in to my seat on the river bank. Silently listening to the game through earbuds, I sat for a couple of hours without seeing anything.

At around 1:30, I had a feeling I was seated in the wrong spot, that maybe I should shift a bit so I could see a little further to the west. I stood and tip-toed a couple of steps up-stream to where I could see around the bend.

As I arrived at that point of visibility, immediately I saw a deer approaching. Then another, and another. The lead deer entered the water and crossed the knee-deep creek to a small gravel island as the other two cautiously observed. Now only thirty yards distant, the leader looked right at me and knew something was wrong. Frozen in alarm mode, the six eyes scanned the scene, watching for any movement. With winds swirling, it was only a minute or two before they caught a puff of my stink and the trio retreated up the steep bank to the southeast. I waited in the area for the remainder of the day, hoping to see a buck following in the footsteps of the other deer. Although the buck failed to show on this day, I was excited to have located such a key spot.

A week of hunting season was now complete, and the returns were marginal at best. After seven days afield, spanning some seventy hours of hunting, my season totals include fourteen deer sightings and zero buck sightings. Not exactly a season to write home about so far.

---Daily total: 3 deer, 0 bucks. Season total: 14 deer, 0 bucks

November 22

The eighth day opened with an inch of new snow on the ground. With clear skies and the air a chilly 17 degrees, finally the season was starting to feel like deer season. Eager to find a buck track to follow, I went back to my old plan to run my regular roads, hoping to find his tracks. With deer populations at an all-time low, the lack of tracks on the ground was striking. After spotting a doe bedded near a main road, it was many miles and ninety-five minutes before I spotted another deer.

There's a deer! In the road. Looks like a buck! Yup. No doubt. My first buck sighting of the season. He bounds down the trail about fifty yards, before taking a left on the first trail heading west.

I juiced the gas and followed around the corner. Around the bend, I followed him down the trail, until his track veered off to the south.

Then I saw him again, standing in the narrow ravine, about 50 yards distant. I got a good look at him, good enough to see that he was just a little guy. Perhaps 120 pounds at best, the little spike-horn carried a mere two inches of antler on his left, and one inch on the right. Not a shooter in any circumstance, but good nonetheless to finally see an antlered buck this season. Hunting in the big woods, you have to appreciate the little things, and that I did. Long may you run, little fella.

For the afternoon hunt, I dropped back into Thunder Canyon with plans to venture across the creek and beyond the water barrier. My makeshift waders invention worked flawlessly as I splashed across the knee-deep gravel-bottomed stream. Emerging on the far side, my feet were dry as a bone. That was easy.

The makeshift waders consisted of an old pair of nylon waders, with the boots removed. The idea was to roll up the lightweight waders and carry them in my pocket until needed. When needed, I'd simply slip the waders over my hunting clothes, then tie down the bottoms of my waders tightly over the top of my waterproof leather hunting boots. A neoprene gaiter would help to cover and seal the transition from boot to water pants. That was the idea anyway. ... And the first test was a success.

With dry feet, I was across the moat and on my way into the deepest woods in the vicinity. After removing the waders, I headed to the southeast and up Fifteen-Point Mountain. Despite the fresh dusting of snow, the forest floor was frozen, crunchy, and noisy. Not much deer sign up on the mountain, but, also, zero human sign in the area. While there wasn't much deer sign around, there was one nice set of buck tracks that passed through. I'll have to get back there, I thought, and someday soon.

Next, I climbed up 100-Sign Mountain, still looking for big tracks. After lingering for a while at the top, I looped back and down into the canyon.

It was a good exploration trip ... until I had to cross the creek again. This time, my crossing place was chosen in the last light of the evening, and unfortunately I chose poorly. Crossing further upstream this time, apparently I underestimated the depth of the flow. Additionally, I failed to notice that the bed of the stream was lined with smooth and slippery rocks the size of kickballs.

While my homemade waders worked fine at the first crossing, where I crossed quickly in shallow water, the second crossing was a different story.

Carefully making my way into the dark current, it was promptly evident this was not going to end well. Within a few steps, the water was above the knee and rising. I felt the first seepage and wanted to hasten my ford. But I couldn't speed it up, unless, of course, I wanted to take a full swim.

With the diligence of a soldier crossing a minefield, I placed each step with extreme caution. Knowing a swim would be a bad thing in an icy river on a 17-degree day, I reminded myself that a slip-up was not an option.

In makeshift waders, this was a tough place to cross the creek.

With my slow and steady crossing, I paid the full price. Half-way across in thigh-deep water, just past the point of no return, the hydraulic pressure exceeded the limits of my boot seals, and the deluge was on. In seconds both boots completely filled with the frigid brew. Staying the course, I made my way carefully and emerged on the north bank, thankfully upright.

It was the soaker supreme. I was swamped, drenched from mid-thigh down to the toes. Fortunately, the warm truck and dry socks were only a quarter of a mile ahead, up the hill. After I sloshed my way up to the truck, I pulled off the boots and poured out the water. As soaked as I was, I almost expected to see minnows swimming out of my boots.

Like many days of hunting in the U.P., this was a day of small victories, minor setbacks, and the cold reality of lessons learned.

---Daily total: 2 deer, 1 buck. Season total: 16 deer, 1 buck

November 23

By the ninth day I was well into the second week of deer camp. It had been a difficult season so far, with lousy hunting weather and few deer sighted. Regardless, I was back at it, up and at 'em and in the woods for first light. Despite the slow start to the season, my spirits were high as I moved into the second week. In my experience, the second week of the season, save for opening day, is usually the most fruitful part of the season.

The snows start flying, the temperatures drop, the hunting pressure falls off, and the deer start moving a little more. In fact, the activity of the season usually seems to peak right around the turkey holiday.

With the mercury holding steady at around 30 degrees, a fresh dusting of snow, and light south winds, this looked to be a better day for hunting. After making my way down the creek and into Thunder Canyon, I returned to the pinch-point bend and constructed a brush blind in the dense undergrowth of the creek bottom. With a little brush clearing, I was able to create clear shooting out to 100 yards in a couple of directions. It looked to be an incredible spot, and the prospects were exciting.

Yet on this day, I had regrets. On my way to the parking spot that morning, I spotted a group of fresh deer tracks headed toward the old logging camp, with a big deer in the mix. It looked to be a perfect setup for tracking. However, rather than taking the track, I played off and took the easy route, choosing instead to sit for a while before heading home early. Wanting to honor my wonderful wife's request, and thinking the snow was too crunchy for effective tracking, I kept the plan to get home and take care of the dog.

Long about mid-afternoon, I got to thinking about my decision and regretted passing up what might be my only chance to track a buck this season. My regrets were magnified when, at around 2:30 p.m., I heard two shots down to the south, toward 100-Sign Mountain and where those tracks were headed. Thinking to myself that I'd have to go and investigate the next day, I had a feeling I'd find a gut pile and Marv's initials carved into a tree somewhere up on the mountain.

I was disappointed that I'd allowed myself to be distracted from the ultimate goal. If I was gonna get that big buck, it was gonna take all of everything I had to give, and now I feared I might never get that opportunity.

Making my way home during prime time, I spotted two does in some oaks just off the road, at right about last shooting light. Even though I took the easy way out, it was another tough day of deer hunting in the U.P.

---Daily total: 2 deer, 0 bucks. Season total: 18 deer, 1 buck

7 DAY OF RECKONING

November 24

The tenth day of the season arrived and things were starting to come together. Extensive scouting during the past week revealed the current core area of a monster buck along with a corresponding network of travel corridors where he recently traveled to leave his calling cards. Including Thunder Canyon, Fifteen-Point Mountain, and 100-Sign Mountain, this vast network of trails was interspersed with some of the finest examples of buck sign ever witnessed. Big scrapes and big rubs were laid down at seemingly every potential spot. No question, there was at least one very large, dominant, and aggressive buck in the neighborhood. Though I now knew the neighborhood he lived in, it was still a pretty big neighborhood in which to search for him.

The question now was whether or not he was still alive. My plan was to keep hanging around his area, which I now knew so well. If he was still alive, sooner or later, I knew he would have to come back. And I was determined to be there when he did.

So the plan for this day was based largely upon the weather forecast. Karl the Weatherman called for partly cloudy skies with a north wind early, then transitioning to a southerly breeze. With temperatures scheduled to climb to 34 degrees and a remnant dusting of snow on the ground, weather wise, this looked to be the best day yet.

Before leaving home, Dawn gave me a big hug and took a moment to wish me well. Knowing full well of my frustration with being distracted the previous day, she told me she'd take care of the dog from here on out. Better yet, she took me by the hand, looked me in the eye, and spoke to me.

"Good luck, Buddy," she said. "I hope you have a great day and that all your hunting dreams come true."

It was the most genuine wishing of well that she had offered all season.

One of many big scrapes near the top of 100-Sign Mountain.

"Thanks for the encouragement," I told her, smiling. "I will have a great day. And this might be THE day. After all, I can walk quiet as a deer now."

Then, off I went, into the forest deep. After my 7 a.m. arrival at the parking spot near 100-Sign Mountain, I headed out on the skid trail, landing at my planned sitting spot after a twenty minute hike. With the wind in my face, I got in quietly and waited near the skid road intersection as the first light of day began to illuminate the sky.

Shooting light came at about 7:40. At 7:50, I looked to the east, and there came a deer, approaching up the skid trail to about forty yards. Since I was standing out in the wide open, and since the wind was puffing more out of the west than north at that moment, the deer promptly busted me. After about forty seconds, the doe bolted to the south, then stopped in the dense balsams where she proceeded to engage in some sort of stomp-fest. On and on she went, stomping and snorting for way too long, making a huge ruckus on an otherwise calm and quiet morning. I was wishing she would just go away. But no. After making such a racket in the brush, that fat old sassy doe stomped her way right back to me, approaching to forty yards again, then added some head-bob moves to her already obnoxious dance. After a few more minutes of this nonsense, she finally turned and heavily bounded away, calling out with a few more emphatic snorts.

See ya. Good riddance. And so much for this spot this morning. Rats.

At 10 a.m. I packed up and headed north for more reconnaissance. With the morning's fresh dusting of snow, I could discern all the travel patterns and recent deer activity. I wanted to see which trails the deer used to drop into Thunder Canyon from the south. At the south rim of the canyon, I listened to the thunder of the falls as I peered down the main game trail to the bottom. Lots of deer tracks here, fresh ones too, though I didn't see any tracks from the big guy.

I descended the steep and densely wooded canyon to the creek bottom, then took a prime trail to the east, past the pinch-point at the bend. All along the way, I kept finding rubs galore. This was certainly a vein among the arteries of the big buck's travel route. At the bend, I found the visuals to be significantly better on the south bank than on the north bank. Without hesitation, I constructed another thicket blind and cleared some openings for shooting. Now this was the place. While only sixty yards from my north shore spot which I'd built the previous day, this place had a much better view. I was certain this would turn out to be one of the best hunting spots ever. I couldn't wait to get back there and sit all day.

At 2:30, after spending a couple of hours constructing a blind at "the best spot ever," I set off upstream, sneaking along the main trail as it passed along the south side of the stream. It was surprising to see how many deer traveled up and down the walls of the canyon and alongside the creek, and how few deer actually crossed the stream. In fact, most of the tracks that actually went into the water were big single tracks, likely those belonging to big bucks as they moved from cover to cover, searching for girlfriends.

At the falls and now northeast of 100-Sign Mountain, I took the nearest trail up the steep bank and headed toward the mountain. It was a challenging climb, steep and rough and jagged under foot, with several places requiring that I drop to my knees to ascend for a while, bulldozer style. Taking my time, I was trying to move with the silence of the wind, my eyes picking apart the forest before me, while my ears scanned for the slightest sound of my quarry.

I should mention here, when I'm approaching a key time or place in my hunting, I often make use of the most important trick up my deer hunting sleeve: *the tip-toe sneak*. Making each step in-time and strictly on my toes, this is the one trick which allows me to regularly get in close to deer. It's not enough just to match the cadence of the deer's stride. The real key is to match the sound of the deer's foot touching the ground. And that can only be done on tip-toes, not with the typical human footfall of heel rolling to toes. In other words, if your heels touch the ground, you lose. It takes practice, balance, and year-round training of the feet and legs in order to have the ability to walk for hundreds of yards on tip-toes. And it's worth all the effort. No doubt, it's the biggest key to my sneak hunting success.

Upon reaching the summit of the saddle between two mountains, on my way to the next mountain I paused to rest the dawgs and get a snack. Wearing my brand new Danner boots for the first time, I quickly removed the slightly stiff sneakers, pulled off my socks, and let my pale-white Fred Flintstone feet see the light of day and feel the fresh air.

Ahhhhh. To air out the dawgs. There's nothing better in the middle of a mighty meander in the deep woods. After that well-deserved pause, I put the leather back on the paws and arose to set off for the conclusion of the day's adventure.

With the wind as advertised and now out of the south, the plan was still on. I would sneak up the northwest corner of the mountain, headed south into the wind, then wait on top in the oaks until dark. With the clock now rolling just past 3 p.m, I had to get at it. Sneaking down to the old skid trail then around the north end of the hill, I was making a good hunt of it. On the trail headed to the top, I found another scrape, and it looked like it'd been touched up earlier in the day. Things were starting to look good.

Quietly, walking every step on my tip-toes and careful to replicate the cadence of the footfalls of an approaching deer, I made my way to the top. Now nearing 4 p.m., I paused at the top, near a large scrape, where I could see down the mountain to the south.

Looking south from atop 100-Sign Mountain, this scene was about to come to life.

In the midst of a relatively calm and quiet day, right away I could hear critters feeding among the acorns and oaks on the hillside below me.

At 4:30 I hear a distinct rustling in the leaves below me. Staunch, I sit there like a dog on point, listening, watching. The forest around me is starting to come to life. Crunch, crunch, crunch. I hear something munching nuts on the hillside below me and to the right, and it's way too big a crunch for a squirrel. Soon, I hear a hoof rake a root, then a couple of footsteps. Incoming. Get ready.

By 5, I'm standing, watching, and hearing all sorts of activity in the dense underbrush below me. At 5:10, I look to the west. There's a deer, a doe, 30 yards away, and heading north. A light puff of the variable wind stops the doe in her tracks. Then she looks my way. Standing in the wide open, she sees me and a staredown ensues. After about 20 seconds, she takes a few quick bounds to the south and ducks out of sight. A moment later, I hear several deer milling around in the aspen saplings, balsams, and oaks below me. Then I see one and another, then several deer, sort of going every which way in bursts of activity about 100 yards down the hill.

Now 5:20, I can hear some serious crashing and commotion in the valley below me. It sounds like there's a buck down there. Then I hear it. The unmistakable sound of a grunting, rutting buck. Then another, and another grunt. Here we go! My heart starts racing. The mountain has come alive and I'm in the middle of the mayhem. For sure, there's a buck down there, rubbing, scraping, just tearing the place up from the sounds of it. With the light fading, I can occasionally see bits and pieces of deer moving about, still eighty to 100 yards distant.

Then the sounds seem to be getting closer. It almost sounds like he's on the trail below me, and with each tree he thrashes, with each hoof that tears at the forest floor, it sounds ever closer.

Light is seriously starting to fade now, and all of this action is starting to take too long to develop. Without any snow on the ground for visual contrast, shapes are beginning to blend into the background and visibility is deteriorating fast. Looking with all my might, I search for the buck.

At some point I consider dropping to a knee for a shooting rest. Not wanting to spook any unseen deer, I think better of it and hold my position. Any shooting I might have would be within seventy-five yards, an easy enough task, even off-hand. And besides, I don't want to compromise my already limited visibility.

With my rifle shouldered, muzzle safely pointed to the ground in front of me, and with the safety off, I'm ready to fire at a moments notice. Yet I still can't see him. I vividly remember thinking to myself: "This is too cruel. I finally get close to a big buck, and now it's gettin' dark and I'm not even gonna see him."

At 5:25 he grunts again and I hear him thrash another tree and paw the ground, still just out of sight. I wait, motionless and silent, heart pounding, listening, watching. Scanning the hillside below me, I expect to see him emerge at any moment into the clearing about sixty yards below me.

Suddenly, movement catches my eye along the side of the clearing, close in front of me. There he is! The first thing I see is his wide, sweeping rack. He's huge! Instantly, I know it's the biggest buck I've ever seen in the big woods, by a wide margin. A huge deer with a rack well over eighteen inches wide, the sight is stunning.

Moving left to right and quartering toward me with his nose to the ground, the buck's head and neck emerge from behind the clump of balsams. He's just thirty yards away and heading right up toward me. In that moment, time stands still. All I can think is: "I've got to get him in the scope. Now."

The instant I see him, I move to raise the scope to my eye. In the same instant, the buck spots my movement, stops, and snaps his head up to look directly at me. Although I'm caught in the act, I steadily continue my motion, just a couple inches from having my scope leveled on the target. Another fraction of a second is all I need. ...

5:30 - There he is. He's huge!!! I raise my gun and he raises his head, looking right at me. Already at half draw, I try to pull up the rest of the way. All I need is one second. Safety off, my eye almost to the scope. ... And he bolts.

Lightning quick, the giant buck turns to run. In the same moment, I point and instinctively pull the trigger. BOOOOM!!! The massive deer thunders down the mountain with the sound of a spooked Clydesdale. After about 100 yards, I hear him stop and the forest falls silent.

Ears ringing, heart pounding, with tears rolling down my cheeks, my heart sank. I knew right away I'd failed. I never saw him through the scope. My shot was ill-advised. More reflex than measured, it was a shot in the dark at a ghost who had already departed. And while tears of sorrow might have been appropriate at that moment, my teary eyes were the result of my scope biting the bridge of my nose in the recoil of my haphazard shot.

5:35 - I knew it was over, never got him in the scope. Inches away, he bolted and reflexively, I touched one off. The recoil, with the gun not firmly planted in my shoulder, drove the scope squarely into my nose, instantly drawing tears. How appropriate.

And there he was, gone. The biggest buck I ever got a chance at in the U.P. and the biggest I've seen in the last 25 years. 30 yards and I blew it. It hurts. So much work, so rare the opportunity. Where do I go from here? At least I know he exists. He's still alive, and I know his home very well. I go try again.

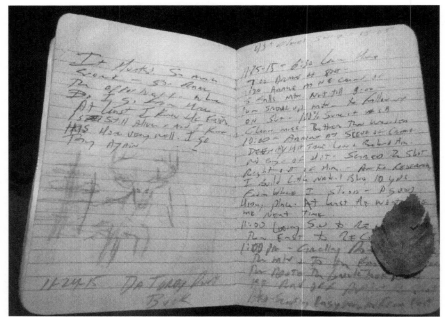

And there he was. … Sketched in my journal on November 24, this is what the huge buck looked like on the first day we met, just before I blew it.

I wanted to break my gun over my knee. Knowing I'd missed, I somberly walked to where the buck had stood, hoping against hope to find the sign of a miracle. Arriving to his lucky place, I scanned the ground with my flashlight, looking for any hair or blood. The only sign I found on the ground were the tracks from his launch pad.

Widening my search, my light scanned to the base of the big oak which was just behind where he stood. And there it was, at the base of the tree, a .30 caliber chunk freshly blasted away. The shot had gone right where I had pointed, about six inches above ground level, directly below and behind where the stag had stood. No question, it was a miss. By a matter of inches, by a fraction of a second, the buck that I had sought for all these years had escaped with his life.

I sat down for a moment, took a drink of water, and listened to the silence. It's hard to describe the feeling of emptiness that one feels when buried in the fog of the ultimate frustration. Hard to describe the depths of disappointment when you fail in the moment you've been working toward for decades. To dedicate a lifetime of effort, only to fail on the grandest stage, there could be no bigger letdown. And I felt all of it.

Walking slowly and dejectedly back to the truck, I could only imagine how it might have felt to come back later in the night, with partners in tow, to share in the victorious and celebratory task of hauling the beast home.

I couldn't help but think of what might have been. This was a buck to write home about, no doubt a buck that would've been the talk of the town. And I could've finally claimed the success I'd worked so hard for. Unfortunately, all of that was not meant to be.

Further along the trail, my mind was flooded with all the what-ifs. What if I'd taken a position just a few steps to the side? What if I'd been posted on one knee, with the scope already to my eye when I heard him coming? What if I'd waited to raise my gun until he looked away?

In hindsight, any and all of the what-ifs sounded better than the cold reality that had come to be. Fact is, I blew it and I knew it. I felt sick.

I drove home in silence. My whole spirit in a state of shock, I felt rather numb. Almost like my whole sensory system had just taken a little bolt of lightning. At this point, I was thankful just to feel my fingers and toes.

At home, I shared the story with Dawn, a story punctuated with grunts, groans, and growls of anguish. Agonizing about the magnitude of my failure, I wondered aloud how long it would take to get another chance of a lifetime. Would I have to wait another twenty-five years?

The wife suggested it might be awhile before he returns to that place, after such a close brush with death. I concurred initially, then reconsidered.

"Big bucks," I noted out loud, "are concerned with just a few things this time of year: finding does, eating, sleeping, and finding does. "If there's a hot doe in there," I went on, "that big buck might be back in no time."

---Daily total: 5 deer, 1 huge buck. Season total: 23 deer, 2 bucks

8 ENCORE TO FAILURE

November 25

On day eleven I headed back to the scene of the previous day's action. Although I knew full well I had missed, as a good sportsman, I needed to go back to survey the scene in the daylight. On the outside chance that something crazy might have happened, I wanted to follow up in the direction that the deer had run off. I just had to be sure that he wasn't lying there dead or wounded somewhere. Arriving at the mountaintop, I replayed the scene and reexamined the evidence. No question, my shot had gone low, and in the daylight, there was zero sign of any hit, except to the base of the tree.

10:00 - Arrive at scene of crime. Definitely hit tree, low and behind him... 100% sure it was a clean miss - better than wounded... Scared the shit right out of him. After research, I build a little natural blind, 10 yards from where I stood. A good hiding place - At least he won't see me next time.

After confirming my failure, I took an hour or so constructing that little hiding spot a few yards from where I'd been standing when I missed. Nestled among some thick balsams at the base of a big double oak, my spot afforded a wide view over the hillside below. If ever our paths crossed again on this mountain, I'd be fully concealed and have prime visibility for shooting. Next time, it would be different.

At around 1 p.m., I headed down the mountain, looking to do some scouting in the direction the buck had gone the previous night. Further east, there was a creek bottom I was hoping to explore later in the day. Circling down the mountain and to the east, I followed the route the buck took as he ran off after the shot. I was slowly and quietly making my way, tip-toeing through the woods, observing the impressive buck sign along the way and carefully surveying the surroundings for any critters.

With temperatures in the mid forties and southwest winds at fifteen to twenty-five, it was a nice day for sneaking and peeking. It's easy to be distracted at an odd time of day when you don't really expect to see anything. But the years have taught me to always be on the ready, to expect to see that big buck at any moment. Measuring my every movement, placing each tip-toed step ever so carefully, I was focused and on full alert.

Scanning the woods before I take the next step, I look ahead to the east and spot a deer, its back shining bright under the mid-day sun. I freeze and watch and wait. Not expecting to see much more than a doe, I wait for it to lift its head. After a minute or two, he brings his head up.

It's him! I bring my gun to my shoulder and peer through the scope. It's him alright. Big buck! Moving from right to left about seventy-five yards in front of me, the buck pauses in his hike up the hill and looks around. With a massive rack of horns resembling a radar dish turning at the airport, his identity is unmistakable.

1:23 - There he is. I don't freakin' believe it. There he is! As I'm sneaking along his escape route, I see him 75 yards up ahead, moving from right to left and up the hill. I bring up the gun. It's thick, popple whips and small oaks between us. Wind is off my right shoulder, out of the west and headed almost right to him.

There he is again. Sketched in my journal on November 25, this was the scene when I crossed paths with the huge buck for a second day in a row.

I look for a rest. Closest thing is a triple birch stump, three steps away. Too risky to move. Then I look for an opening to shoot through. Almost too thick for a shot. His nose goes up and tests the wind. He looks around. He could bolt at any second. I look for an opening and find one, about an inch wide at 75 yards. He smells the air again, and I decide, 'I gotta go.'

Looking through the scope, I pick apart the woods between us and carefully search for a clear line of fire. I stand tall, crouch down, lean left and lean right, all the time looking for an opening. The buck seems to be getting nervous. I see his nose go to the sky, then he scans the surroundings. He looks my way. Although he doesn't see me, with the wind blowing from me to him, I know he could spook at any moment. Desperately, I search for a shot. And there, I find a narrow seam in the tree screen. It's not much, but I can clearly see the fur covering his shoulder. Without further thought, I hold steady and squeeze the trigger. Boooom!

With the sound of the blast, the deer gets low, scoots forward, and disappears. Did I get him? I lean to and fro, looking for any sign of him. My inner voice asks again, did I get him? Then I see a doe take off, running east, and the big buck follows. I follow suit and join the chase, running about fifty yards southeast, before pausing at the edge of a clearing.

And here he comes, running across in front of me, left to right at fifty yards. At first sight, I pull up my rifle. Instantaneously, I look through the scope to acquire the target. Finger already on the trigger, safety off, I find the deer, take aim … and he's gone. In the moment it takes for the word "go" to travel from my brain to my finger, the deer disappears with one bound into a deep ravine and vanishes like smoke in the wind.

I run about 50 yards to the clearing, and there he is, running across in front of me. One bound, I bring the gun up. Two bounds, find him in the scope. Three bounds, set to squeeze the… and he drops down the back of a steep hill. Gone.

Once again, a split second and a matter of inches was the barrier that separated me from success. In the moment I took to be sure of my aim, the buck slipped away, like a magician behind a cape. I never fired my shot, the target having made like a football held by Lucy for the kick, pulled away from Charlie at the last second.

And that was it. Over. He was gone. And the windy woods fell silent. With only ruffled leaves and scattered dirt to mark his trail of retreat, once again that sinking feeling set in. From the looks of it, the first shot had not made it through to the target. And unfortunately, the second shot never flew.

I could barely believe it. How on earth could I get a chance at the biggest buck ever, two days in a row, and blow it both times? How could I be so lucky and so unlucky all at once. How utterly and completely maddening.

This small tree was the only thing I hit when I had a second chance at the huge buck.

Though it was clear I'd missed, I went to the place where the buck stood when I shot to look for any sign of a hit. Like the previous day, I found where he stood along with his tracks where he ran away. And like the day before, there was absolutely no sign of hitting the deer.

What I did find was a maple sapling, a little bigger around than my thumb, which was cleanly and freshly sawed off by a bullet. It was just a few inches below his chest when he stood there. The sapling must have fallen on his back when I shot it out from under him. That had to be what caused him to drop low and scoot forward after the shot. And once again, it was obviously a clean miss. Better that, I reassured myself, than wounding him.

Dejected, I sat down for a drink of water. As I wiped the sweat from my brow with my bandana, I felt the sting of a wound. I looked at my handkerchief and spotted blood. Son of a gun. I had drawn blood after all. My own damn blood. This time, instead of getting bitten in the nose by the scope, the optics kicked me in the head, slicing my forehead open right between the eyebrows. How fitting. And why not? I had already shed plenty of sweat and tears.

I spent the remainder of the day attempting to sort out his tracks in the damp leaves. It was a hopeless and fruitless task. At the end of the day, for the second straight time, I drove home in stunned silence, defeated.

---Daily total: 2 deer, 1 huge buck. Season total: 25 deer, 3 bucks

9 BACK TO THE DRAWING BOARD

November 26

On to the twelfth day and it's back to the old drawing board. Thanksgiving Day, and I forgo the carving board. At 6:30 a.m. I'm back on the road, headed for the woods. Through the darkness, I made my way back to the mountain. Although I had no expectations of seeing that big buck three days in a row, I figured I had best go back to the same area, if for no other reason than to play defense.

On the way in, I bumped one deer near the beaver marsh, then bumped several more as I eased up into the edge of the oaks. Dammit. Even with a good wind, even in the dark, I'd pushed too far, too fast, and was far too noisy, spooking my quarry. I remembered my brother's tale from earlier in the season, when he had spooked several deer near his stand, then stayed put and soon shot a nice buck. I decided to stay put for a while.

As daylight filled the hills, I found myself stationed about halfway between the two locations where I had my chances the previous two days. At the lower end of the oak ridge I took my position in a dense clump of balsams, facing north into the wind.

At 8:20, two deer approached from the northwest, headed right at me. Moving steadily, the lead deer, a fawn, approached to seven yards before pausing. With the doe right behind at twelve yards, they both locked up and began searching for me. They seemed to have entered my scent cone and sensed that danger lurked nearby. For nearly 5 minutes, they looked and sniffed and stared, but never saw me or spooked.

Fully concealed in my pine blind, they never picked me out, even at such close range. Eventually, they turned and returned to where they had come from, tails out but not up. At 9, the rain began to fall. Still I held my position. I was hoping the deer would be on the move before the impending storm.

10:20 Just had a red squirrel come up to inches from my face. After several false starts, he popped up and looked me in the eye at about 16 inches away. I talked to it, said hello & on & on, and it seemed interested. No spookin'- just looking and listening curiously. It hung around for a minute or so, then went on its way without so much as a squawk.

The day started getting pretty drippy at around 10:30 so I decided to take a hike. Walking the skid trail in my poncho, the day was getting progressively dreary, the drips now evolving into a downright downpour. By 1 p.m. the rain was transitioning to a wet and heavy snow.

At 3, the ground was starting to turn white, and the collar of my wool coat had turned into a sponge. The poncho is good in a pinch. But with the hood down, a must for vision and hearing, the hat and exposed coat collar serve to sponge and wick a good deal of moisture. That sponge and wicking effect also works near the ankles and wrists, especially during prolonged exposure to heavy precipitation, and I was feeling all of it. It was a cold, damp, miserable day.

All cold and wet, hunkering under a hemlock, I thought about the comforts of a warm home on Thanksgiving Day. A part of me wanted to give up this whole foolish hunting thing and get back home to my family for some turkey and stuffing. If only things had worked out differently on one of the last two days, then I'd be there now. But no. Lucky me, out there enduring the worst of the possible elements. The joys of hunting.

By 4, I was back in my pine tree hideout, on the south slope of the mountain. An hour into the afternoon sit, two deer came down from the north, caught my wind, then promptly reversed course. With fresh tracking snow on the ground and a deep chill settling into my bones, I decided to end the day by sneaking southwest and into the wind.

About 100 yards down the line, I paused to scan the surroundings and spotted a deer approaching. Then another. The two does passed by without alarm at less than twenty-five yards. Like two ships passing on a cold and sloppy night, we each headed to where the other had come from.

---Daily total: 4 deer, 0 bucks. Season total: 29 deer, 3 bucks

November 27

The thirteenth day of the season looks to be, weather-wise, perhaps the best day yet. With three to four inches of powdery snow, I finally had a tracking snow to work with. Driving through the darkness, I made my way along the road near Thunder Canyon, looking for a fresh buck track.

Just before first light, and bingo, I found a buck track. Near the old logging camp, the buck had crossed through the notch between mountains and headed east, right up the trail where I had seen the one early on the second morning of the season.

Thinking I might want to take this track later, I decided to hop out and walk the track for a short ways to investigate further. I had backtracked less than fifty yards when I found two fresh rubs, complete with shavings on top of the snow, made by this buck within the last hour. It was a good hot track. Maybe not a huge buck, but not a little one either. Definitely a candidate to consider.

My next stop was a return to my favorite mountain. By now, the spot had earned a new name: Thirty-Point Mountain, as in the song, "Da Turdy Point Buck." How could I call it by any other name? After having witnessed the scene come to life twice in two days, the prophecy was fulfilled. It was just like the old song says: "And dare e was ... gone."

Arriving at the parking spot, I was the first guy in this morning. I made tracks through the unbroken snow as I headed to the mountain. On the way in, I spotted two deer bedded about forty yards off the skid trail, just watching through the snow-laden forest as I snuck past. With the thick snow splattered to every branch and twig, the deer displayed an unusual sense of security, standing pat as I stopped, observed them, then moved on.

Rounding the east end of the mountain, I spooked several deer off the shoulder of the hill, all of which bounded down to the north. Continuing west around the north end of the hill, I planned to circle the mountain and

When the snow sticks to the trees, you have to look closely to spot bedded deer.

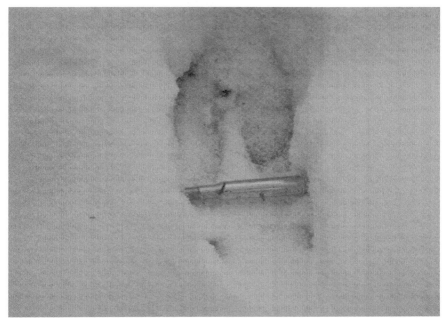

Smoking hot in a fresh powder snow, this big track was a good one to follow.

hoped to find the huge tracks of that big buck. After continuing west for about a half mile, I turned and completed the mountain loop. There had been a few tracks up there this morning, but no big bucks around.

Back to the truck by 9:30, I hopped in and headed back to pick up the buck track I'd found earlier in the morning. The excitement was building as I made my way to that smoking hot, 100 percent for sure buck track. While it might not have been huge, it was a good one, and headed directly to an area I was familiar with.

Rather than parking right on the track, I parked about a half mile away, then took a cross-country shortcut to where I thought he was headed. Expecting the buck to cross the creek, I brought along the waders and stashed them down by the water for later use. I made my way up the hill, then on to where I found the track earlier in the day.

At 10 I picked up the track and began the journey. Right away, the excitement surged through my body. Above all other hunting experiences, this is what I live for, taking a hot track in the snow on a brisk day to wherever the buck chooses to go. What could be better?

Moving steadily, I knew he was at least a couple of hours ahead of me by now. Through the valley we went, southeast, then turning southwest and up through a saddle between two mountains. Passing through the gulch then on toward the creek crossing, I cautiously followed the spoor.

Nearing the old logging camp, I noticed another track crossing from the west. It's an even bigger track, wider, and sloppy looking in the snow with a broad plodding stride. Better yet, this bigger track is most certainly fresher than the one I'd followed to this point. Without a second thought, my focus shifted to the new track.

Headed east, I got right on it, assuming he'd gone down to cross the river. Not fifty yards along the track, I found where the buck hooked a decent-sized sapling. Leaving tree shavings atop the snow along with distinct antler imprints, I knew I was onto a real good one. Trending east and up a small rock knob, the buck led me through a dense tangle of evergreens.

Pushing through the thicket, it was nearly impossible to move quietly. About fifty yards in, I heard what sounded like the crack of brush and a deer bounding away. I wasn't too worried about that, thinking the buck was still well ahead of me. The buck's tracks then emerged into an open stand of oaks adjacent to the rock knob, and into a plethora of other tracks where multiple deer had been foraging in the field of nuts.

Following the big buck track among the herd was child's play, his large track easily recognizable among the smaller, average-sized tracks. Ranging from one productive tree to the next, the buck stopped occasionally to dig up an acorn. In several places I noticed the imprint of his antler tips poking into the snow as his lips pressed to the forest floor for a nut to crunch.

While subtle, antler marks left behind when the deer nosed into the snow for acorns can tell you much about the animal you are tracking.

Judging by the antler marks spanning more than sixteen inches, it looked like this track might belong to the big guy.

I took a moment and visually scanned the forest around me. After a few minutes, I continued on the track. Carefully, I placed each tip-toed step, watching all around me for any hint of a deer. The buck wound his way through the oaks, around the knob, then turned and headed up hill. Creeping silently, one step at a time, I snuck up the hill. Nearing the top, I rounded a boulder, and there it was. Right atop the knob, under a big pine, a fresh bed, empty. I snuck over to the nest and found the buck's exit tracks.

Dammit! I blew it again. He was bedded in the perfect spot. And I was imperfect. I'd pushed too far, too fast, and I bumped him. I should've looped around the downwind side of the thicket instead of making the noise of pushing through. Rats! Now it was gonna get tough, real tough.

Back on his track I found he immediately set out to backtrack himself. Crossing through the logging camp and right down our tracks from minutes ago, he continued east to where he had come from. In dogged pursuit, I trudged on. With snow stuck to all the branches, in short order I was well camouflaged, covered in snow and looking like a small sasquatch in the coat of a powered sugar donut.

And we were off to the races. It was a noisy snow to track in, with a few inches of powder covering a woods coated in a layer of ice. Not far into the track I found where he had waited and listened for my approach, before he broke away in another burst of bounds. Soon we were in the next creek bottom, still following in the opposite direction of his previous tracks.

At the creek crossing, I contemplated surrender, or at least getting back to the truck for a reset. Instead, I chose to push on to parts unknown. As it turns out, that was another mistake on my part.

After hopping the creek, we continued upstream through the bottom tangle, before crossing again, then heading north up the hill. As we started to go up, I was thinking I might get another chance. I paused for lunch, then continued onward. About a quarter mile after lunch, I found where he had bedded, then got up and walked back toward me. Again, I could see where he had waited and listened for my approach, and again he had bounded away.

The cat and mouse marathon was now under way. Up and down, left and right we went, I following, he leading, on a romp through his favorite haunts. Along the way, I noticed multiple signpost rubs, confirming this was a regular route for the big buck. After a couple of miles of winding through the woods, the buck set out on a north heading, crossed a road, then headed up into the next range of mountains.

Again, I considered leaving the track, but instead pressed on, hoping I might catch him looking back from the next mountaintop. Up and up we went until we reached the pinnacle. By this time, it was getting pretty late and my legs were getting worn down.

When he dropped off the mountain range to the east, just before dark, I knew it was over. Now several miles from the truck, I had my work cut out for me just to get back to the vehicle.

Defeated again, I questioned my wisdom in carrying on the chase so far. You just never know when you might get lucky, so I stayed with it as far as I could. I should have known better. As it is, if you're tracking a buck and you don't get him on your first encounter, the job can get real tough, real quick, even in the perfect conditions. And the risk you run in pressing on regardless is that with each step, the likelihood increases that you might be chasing the deer into the range of another hunter. On this day, with no snow falling and a shallow powder on top of frozen leaves, the conditions made it nearly impossible to stalk with any degree of stealth. It was a fool's errand indeed.

Regardless of the tough conditions, it was still my best chance at tracking this season. And I blew it within the first half hour. He was right in front of me, looped into a bed behind the thicket on the riverbank above the oaks. I should have looped around downwind, found no tracks out, then done the super slow death creep until I spotted him. It was a big guy, maybe THE big guy. And I blew it before I knew it.

Sometimes it's best to call off the chase, even in fresh snow.

Meanwhile, after that fool's errand, my legs were so blown out, I knew it would take days to recover. I should have given it up after I jumped him the first time. In poor sneaking conditions, I should have known it would be way too noisy to sneak up on him. After exerting way too much energy on a wild-goose chase, I quickly realized I was way too tired to do any more tracking any time soon.

---Daily total: 5 deer, 0 bucks. Season total: 34 deer, 3 bucks

10 END OF A SEASON

November 28

Like clockwork, for the fourteenth consecutive day, I was on the road well before daylight. With only three days left of the season, fatigue had now fully set in to my aging bones. In a word, I was exhausted. With no time to quit, three simple words were ringing in my ears: Don't give up. So I pressed on.

Again, I chose to park at the Thirty-Point Mountain spot and head up that way. I really wanted to park in a different spot, but I chose the main parking spot for one reason: defense. Being the weekend, I wanted to be sure to discourage any other would-be hunters who might consider parking in "my" spot. I hogged the spot and hoped any others would pass by.

On the trail, I walked the mile back to the mountain in the dark, covering the distance in about twenty minutes. I took a position near where I had missed the big buck the second time and waited for daylight to develop. At around 8:15 two deer passed by about forty yards to the west, then headed north. After another cold hour of waiting I decided to move on.

Passing by Thirty-Point Mountain, I continued down the old logging road, then east for another mile to the Fifteen-Point Mountain area. To my delight, there was zero sign of any other hunters having passed this way. Better yet, as I climbed the southeast slope of the hill, the amount of deer sign was increasing. Nearing the location of my fabulous hunt of 2013, I found where a big buck had crossed several times in the past few days.

At 10 o'clock, I took a seat near an intersection of runways where the big buck had passed. It was a brisk morning, clear with temperatures holding steady around twelve degrees and three to four inches of fresh snow stuck to everything. A gorgeous winter day. Sitting on a fallen log in a saddle between the main mountain and a side-hill knob, I was overlooking a prime crossing in a large stand of mature oaks. It was a beauty of a spot.

Listening to the Ishpeming High School state championship football game on my radio and earbuds, my attention was called when I heard a deer snort to the south. Moving through the snow-studded forest, one, then two deer approached. The doe and fawn got to about forty yards away, then the doe got nervous. They hung out for several minutes, the doe's head bobbing, searching with her nose for the source of the awful smell that now offended her olfactory. With a gust of wind at my back, they solved the riddle and retreated to where they had come from.

By 12:30, the Ishpeming football team had claimed yet another state championship, and my time for sitting and shivering had come to an end. I stood to take a pee and stepped into the sun. That warm sun sure felt good on a cold winter day.

Soon after the game, I was making my way up the mountain. At 2:30, with legs still burning from the previous day's folly, I decided to abandon my plan to climb Fifteen-Point Mountain on this day. I was just too fatigued to scale another mountain.

I lingered in the area between mountains until light began to fade then started back for the truck. Turning back to the west, I slowly trudged through the snow, pausing frequently on my three-mile uphill hike back to the rig. It was a long walk out.

Upon arriving at the truck, I noticed a piece of paper pinned under the windshield wiper. I took it up and read it. This is what it said:

Hi-
I believe we are looking for the same buck out on the mountain. He is hard to find.... Saw him 3 times, no shot. Was it you I saw by the ponds last week? (I was up on the rock)
If you get him, I would love to hear the tale. Also, we should talk about next season if you plan on hunting this side of the mountain again. Pretty much all public land over here but it would be nice to not be stepping on each other's toes.
Best of luck to you AND the mountain buck.
-Ian 906-000-0000

Instantly, I knew this tale was more than just my own. I was no longer chasing any ordinary deer. I was in pursuit of a legend. Then and there, his name was revealed to me: the Legend of Thunder Canyon. Sure, he was a mountain buck, but his range covered many mountains. The one common denominator in the land of the Legend was Thunder Canyon, a corridor linking together all of his favorite locales.

With a home range covering at least nine square miles, the Legend obviously worked hard to defend many mountains: Thirty-Point, Fifteen-Point, Muzzleloader, and the Twin Mountains included.

He was a legend of many mountains indeed, and as it turns out, he was known far and wide. I could only imagine the tales other hunters had to tell about this buck, and I could barely imagine how this one deer had gotten so lucky, so many times.

And so it is, the Legend of Thunder Canyon came to be.

---Daily total: 4 deer, 0 bucks. Season total: 38 deer, 3 bucks

November 29

With the dawn of the fifteenth day of the season, it was getting down to the nitty-gritty. With legs still worn down from a season of stalking, I was rolling the roads, looking for a fresh track to take. On the way to Thunder Canyon, I saw four deer and several sets of tracks, but nothing I wanted to follow. With the snow now three days old, it was nearly impossible to decipher fresh tracks from old.

Along the way of my travels through the two-tracks, I ran into my old friends Big John and Little John. I pulled alongside, and we cut the engines to chit-chat. Turns out, this year had been kind to those guys. Big John got a nice nine-pointer on opening day, in the next mountains to the north. Meanwhile, Little John was able to tag a nice eight-pointer late in the first week near my Secret Lake spot. Yeah, that spot, the place I gave up on after seeing the wolves on the first day. Nothing like a little salt in the wound.

Skilled and experienced hunters, these guys tag nice bucks seemingly every year. And big bucks too. Not surprisingly, in 2014, they found success as well, with Big John tagging a nice ten-point, and Little John harvesting a decent eight-point. And that's not to mention the double play that Little John pulled in 2012 when he took a big ten-point on the first day and a dandy eleven-point in the second week.

It was nice to see the fellas again this year. We talked for nearly an hour before we all decided to get back to hunting. We wished each other well and went on our ways. Despite the slight sting of envy, I was happy for those guys. A father and son team, they are as good of hunters as you can find, and they do it the old-fashioned way, tracking, stalking, sneaking, and still-hunting. More importantly, they're just genuinely good people, not anything like some of the territorial and ornery hunters who patrol the areas surrounding their little pieces of private property closer to town.

Later, I parked near Thunder Canyon, then made my way down to the creek and headed upstream. After sneaking about a mile along the creek, I reached the old logging camp. Taking a perch overlooking a well-worn crossing, just up from the water, I settled into a seat on a log among the tall oaks and pines. I thought about my season and considered what I had learned this year. Several things stuck out right away, and I jotted them down in my field notes.

1. *Few deer actually cross the creek.*
2. *Bucks regularly cross the stream at key spots.*
3. *Hunt Secret Lake more in the first week. (Thanks Little John.)*
4. *Hunt Thunder Canyon after November 20.*
5. *If you find fresh buck tracks in the snow, slow down and think about it. If possible, try to circle downwind.*
6. *If you jump him out of his bed and conditions are not perfect, forget it. You'll never see him again that day, and you risk chasing him into harm's way.*
7. *Hunt the key crossings on weekends, especially after fresh snow, when other hunters will be out chasing.*
8. *Not all snow is created equal. Some is good for tracking, some is not.*

Sitting until dark, I saw nothing moving this afternoon. Now it's down to the final countdown.

---Daily total: 4 deer, 0 bucks. Season total: 42 deer, 3 bucks

November 30

It was the sixteenth and last day of the firearm season. After that Ian fella left the note on my truck, I decided to leave that parking spot to him for the last two days. No sense in playing defense and parking in a less-strategic spot. Instead, I parked in an obscure place and approached Thirty-Point Mountain from a different direction, this time with the wind in my favor.

Making my way down the creek, upon reaching the bend, I turned up and into the hills. Scouting some new terrain details in Thunder Canyon, I found some oak stands that had recently been torn up by hungry deer. There was a good crop of acorns up there, and the tracks indicated the big buck had been there recently. Moving further uphill, I found his fresh bed atop a rock knob with a strategic view. The bed had been vacated earlier in the day. It was obvious no one was gonna sneak up on him up there.

After a mid-day forest picnic, I began to make my way to the secret trail that leads to the top of Thirty-Point Mountain. My last stand for the season would be made at the scene of my great failure. It was a scene likely to haunt my dreams for a long time.

Sitting in my little brush blind in the balsams under the oaks at the top of the mountain, my encounters with the Legend played back in my mind over and over. I tried to clear my mind and considered possible plans for next season. Again, I took a moment to write down my ideas.

1. *Sit noisy days. Track while it's snowing and just after the snow.*
2. *Set up sitting spots or brush blinds for noisy and wet days.*
3. *Sneak through the mountains on damp and quiet days.*
4. *Sit at main crossings on weekends or after snow. Get in early.*

Three hours passed and by the time last light faded, I had seen nothing. Nada. A perfect bookend to the firearm season. As I had begun the season, so too did I end the season, with a day of zero deer sighted.

Making my way back to the truck after dark, I was almost thankful the season was over. If nothing else, physically, it was a relief to finally take a break. Similarly, my mind needed some rest. The season was over, but hopefully, I was far from being done deer hunting this year. In just four days, the ten-day muzzleloader season was scheduled to get under way.

---Daily total: 0 deer, 0 bucks. Season total: 42 deer, 3 bucks

****

<u>2015 Firearm Season Stats:</u>
42 deer sightings, 16 from road.
3 buck sightings, 1 from road.
14.5 days hunted = 2.89 deer/day
145 hours hunted = 1 deer per 3.46 hours
1 buck per 4.83 days = 1 buck per 48.3 hours hunted

****

11 A NEW SEASON BEGINS

Now, it might seem a little crazy to dedicate so much time and effort to such a difficult task. Some might even say it's a waste of time. But this is what I do. As an artist, writer, photographer, adventurer, and outdoorsman, these adventures that I embark upon serve as the foundation upon which I create. This comprehensive and exhaustive research is essential in order to experience and share these extraordinary stories of the woods. So, onward I trudge.

Despite my complete exhaustion from a sixteen-day marathon of a season, the show must go on. With only three days to rest and recover from the intense firearm hunt, the muzzleloader season seemed to come too soon. The weather still refused to turn to winter, the woods yet to fill with snow.

Somewhere along the line during the gun season, my dear wife suggested I might want to try scouting in the hills closer to home. During her walks with our beloved pound hound, she'd stumbled upon lots of tracks in the hills, including some big buck tracks. I trusted her judgment, as I knew she was well-equipped to observe and differentiate between tracks. Hanging around with a guy like me for a couple of decades, a gal gets to spend plenty of time in the woods. And she's sharp, pays attention to the details, and knows what a big track looks like.

On December 2, I followed her advice and scouted those hills closer to home. Climbing up the ridge, I arrived at a well-known plateau filled with mature oaks. In the summer and early fall, I'd noticed the carpet of acorns during my hikes with the hound. In places, the acorns were so numerous, the forest floor was dangerous to walk on, like treading on a carpet of marbles. Of course, this was no secret to the critters, and all of the deer from the surrounding hills were now coming to pasture.

Just off the main trail, I found the first key sign. It was a nice rub with an accompanying scrape at the base of the tree. Thirty yards down the trail, I found another rub, then another cluster of rubs. Around the bend and heading down the ridge to the south, the trail was adorned with three nice-sized scrapes. She was right. There was a good buck hanging around.

The next day, I set up a trail camera in the core of the oaks on the hill. I was determined to find out who was claiming this turf. By the looks of it, it was more than a spike-horn raising trouble in my neck of the woods.

In my imagination, I pictured a nice eight-point up on the hill, watching and listening as I ignorantly headed down the highway, day after day, to parts unknown chasing a silly deer. He had me figured out. Safe up on the hill and just down the road, he watched me come and go like clockwork. Oh the folly.

Game on: December 4

Opening Day of the muzzleloader season and like clockwork I'm off to parts unknown, chasing some silly deer. My first choice for the season is to return to Thirty-Point Mountain. After sneaking around the east end of the hill, I make my way to the top and settle in for the day. I hold my position at the top all through the day and my vigil yields nothing, zero deer. It's another slow start to another season.

---Daily total: 0 deer, 0 bucks. Season total: 0 deer, 0 bucks

December 5

For the second day of the season, I decided to scout the northeast end of Thunder Canyon, looking for a place to set up the tent blind. On the way to the spot, I saw two deer off the road. At least I wouldn't be shut out for the day. At 11 o'clock, I located a perfect place, in the oaks on the extreme northeast rim of the canyon.

Now, setting up and waiting it out in a tent blind is not necessarily my favorite way to hunt, but at this point in the season, I was wiling to try just about anything. Having worn my legs nearly to stubs while tramping the hills for the past two weeks, it was almost time to take a nice cozy seat. Considering a weather forecast that called for dry leaves, followed by torrential rains, followed by cold biting winds, followed by a deep freeze, the idea of setting up a warm dry shelter suddenly seemed quite inviting. With the less-than-optimal weather conditions hindering my preferred hunting techniques, the plan to wait it out in comfort was looking like the only good option.

At noon, I found myself all set up as I zipped myself into the blind to wait. With a temperature near fifty degrees, bright sunshine and the woods bone dry, it seemed like a good day to sit. No sense in even trying to be sneaky. Too noisy of a day. And with winds up to thirty-five miles per hour, shelter from the biting wind was welcomed. I pulled my notebook from my pocket, and made some scribbles.

Fresh rubs and a fresh scrape on the trail in. It's an easy spot, super easy, only about 200 yards from the truck. But I think it's good & there's a buck hanging around. I'm gonna get him, right here. It sure feels nice sitting in a comfy chair, out of the wind, and sorta in the sun. And I can do other stuff while hunting - like writing, and thinking, and listening to tunes. If this works, I might like it. Toughest part is staying warm. And staying awake.

I sat until dark, stayed awake in fact, and wound up seeing zero deer.

---Daily total: 2 deer, 0 bucks. Season total: 2 deer, 0 bucks

December 6

On the third day of season, my best judgment gave to me a warm seat under a tree. After strategically shifting the tent blind about five feet just before daylight, I settled in for the day's sit along the north rim of Thunder Canyon. I sat all day, dawn to dusk, and surprisingly, stayed wide awake and warm. The day didn't seem to drag on too bad, despite the fact I never saw a single lousy deer all day long. Not sure if I really like this idea of sitting in a blind all day. At least I got to listen to the Lions and da Packers on da radio.

---Daily total: 0 deer, 0 bucks. Season total: 2 deer, 0 bucks

12 TIME FOR A NEW PLAN

December 7
On the fourth day, I was simply hoping to see a single deer in the woods. So, for the first time ever, I hiked up an overlooked hill closer to home and arrived at the top before first light. Although I spooked a few deer in the dark on my way in, I was confident I would see something.

My hunch proved true shortly after daylight when I saw a deer sneak by to the east of me, headed south and up to the oaks. A short while later, I had two deer approach from the west. In the frozen leaves, I could hear them coming some time before they appeared. Making their way right to me, they finally reached their destination, a mere twenty-five yards west of me. There, under a grove of ultra-productive oaks, the twin button bucks proceeded to munch a lunch of acorns for nearly twenty minutes.

While I didn't see any antlered bucks, it was one of the best mornings I had all season. With deer showing up every half hour starting at 8, I saw five deer by 10, more than I'd seen in the previous three days combined.

After the last deer of the morning cleared, I made my way about 100 yards up the ridge to check the trail camera. Looking at the fresh buck sign on the way, I expected to see some photos of a buck. Probably an eight-point, I thought.

At the camera, the ground was fully torn up by the many deer that must have visited. I cracked the shell and found that the camera had recorded hundreds of photos in the past four days. Excited to see the results, I pulled the memory card and placed it in my pocket camera for a quick review.

Doe, doe, doe and fawn, doe, does and fawns, fawns, does, does, fawns, does and fawns, does, and on and on hundreds of times as I scrolled through the pictures. Doe, does, does, does and fawns, more does and fawns, and wait. What was that?

Scanning through the photos, I went back a few frames and there he was. I got him! It was a nice buck. A real nice one. A beauty of a 9-pointer, it looked like a three-year-old.

On a brief detour, the big buck had bullied his way into the scene at 8:37 yesterday morning. As the submissive other deer looked on, the big guy hung around for about seven minutes, making a dozen selfies while he pawed the turf. As quickly as he showed up, he was off on his way, continuing on his regular course of travel. And where was I while all this was going on? Oh yeah, I was miles away sitting in a silly tent blind all day. What a joke.

For the afternoon hunt, I returned to the saddle in the ridge, where the nine-point had done the selfies the day before. Starting at 4, I had deer all around me, seven in all, and they hung around till dark. Although I didn't see the big buck on this day, I figured he'd be back soon.

---Daily total: 12 deer, 0 bucks. Season total: 14 deer, 0 bucks

December 8

Having discovered a big buck closer to home, my focus quickly shifted. While this nine-point was no match for the Legend of Thunder Canyon, it was a buck any hunter would be thrilled to get. All of a sudden, I'd found another buck to hunt and I was feeling pretty good about my chances.

This buck made a good living hiding out in the hills closer to home.

After I'd worked myself to the bone during the firearm season, a few days of easy hunting close to camp seemed like an appealing proposition.

So for the fifth day of the season, my plan was to return to the nearby ridge for another round of morning and evening hunting. It felt nice, walking out the door in the morning and not having to drive for nearly an hour to get to my spot. It was almost like the old days, back on the farm. And it sure was exciting walking up that hill, knowing there was big buck up there, somewhere.

Sitting from 7:25 to 10, the morning hunt produced seven deer and zero bucks. In the afternoon, I returned to the same spot to see five deer and again, no bucks. It was a fun day, with deer all around me from 4 until dark. My spot was a dandy with good visuals and excellent concealment. Sitting on the ground the whole time with deer in close proximity all around me, amazingly, none of the deer ever spooked.

Now this was my kind of hunting. For the second straight day I'd seen twelve deer, more than I'd seen in any one day all year. It was another fun hunt after many days of seeing next to nothing.

---Daily total: 12 deer, 0 bucks. Season total: 26 deer, 0 bucks

December 9

The sixth day of my muzzleloader season started, again, up on the oak ridge close to camp. I arrived at my hiding spot at 7:25, well before shooting light. This time it was a good sneak in, and with the leaves damp on a warm morning, I didn't spook any. By 8, there were deer all around me, randomly foraging in the abundant acorns. Within an hour, I had seen ten deer, all baldies. Then the action for the morning shut down.

Will he ever come back? I believe he will. He has to, right?

In the afternoon, I returned to my ridge-top sitting spot. Between 3:30 and dark, I watched a doe and two fawns feeding together, and nothing else. This is tough.

---Daily total: 13 deer, 0 bucks. Season total: 39 deer, 0 bucks

December 10

After three consecutive days of watching the same woods and seeing only does and fawns, I opted for yet another new plan for the season's seventh day. Time was winding down, and I felt I could nary afford to spend too much time sitting in one spot.

This time, on her way to work, my lovely wife dropped me off a few miles from my truck. The plan was to hunt my way back to my vehicle, exploring the terrain on the way. From the outset, it was a soggy and drippy day, a good day for sneak hunting. For first light, I took a seat just off the main trail where several runways cross.

At 9 a.m. I looked to the south and saw a large animal approaching quickly through the rain. I raised my gun from under my poncho and moved it into position as the medium-sized brown critter rounded the bend at a trot.

A wolf? Nope ... it's a coyote. And here comes another, and another, all trotting up the trail toward me. As the trio drew closer, I noticed a straggler bringing up the rear. They paused to shake the hydro from their hides then continued on. Steadily trotting right at me, the pack was quickly in to forty yards before they all put on the binders. In the still and damp morning air, they had hit my scent cone. Sniffing the air, noses to the sky, the group tried to find the source of the stink.

After a minute or two of looking around and licking the air, the leader took a left and led the next two on a detour and up the hill to the west. A moment later, the straggler took a right and curled around to the east.

Suddenly surrounded, for a moment I felt like the hunted, yet I had no fear. Despite tales of the big bad wolf, a wild canine is nothing to be afraid of. Instead, I was moved by a feeling of awe, witnessing such a rare and beautiful natural scene. With fur fully bristled up against the cold rain, they looked large and luxurious. It was fascinating to see these social animals work their magic together.

Later on, after hiking through several miles of prime deer country, I finally spotted the first deer of the day. A little later I caught another fleeting glimpse of another fleeing deer, and that was it for the day.

The scene where four coyotes approached and passed by in the rain.

Completing my scouting mission, I was disappointed to find not one, but two baited shack blinds less than a quarter mile from my secret oak ridge. My excitement for this new spot was suddenly snuffed. That changes everything. And I thought I had the place to myself. Not so. I guess it's back to the drawing board. Cold, wet, exhausted, and dejected, I took a moment to vent in my field journal.

So tired. Exhausted. Tired of hunting. Burned out. Two years straight of hard work, and nothing... Not even that much fun. No pictures, no nothing, except sore legs, sore back, and 165 lbs. of frustration. I quit. Three more days & then I'm done, maybe for good! See ya fool's errand, see ya wild goose chase, see ya wasted time. I got better things to do. I'm goin home!

Already down in the dumps, I marched down the hill and headed home.

---Daily total: 2 deer, 0 bucks. Season total: 41 deer, 0 bucks

December 11

By the eighth day of the season, I could feel my resolve starting to wear thin. Discouraged by the evidence of other hunters in the hills close to home, I decided to head back into the deep woods. Several miles inland at an elevation a few hundred feet above Lake Superior, I found two inches of fresh snow on the ground.

Looking for a smoking hot buck track, I made my way by truck through some of my favorite mountain roads. As usual, there were very few tracks to be seen in many miles of cruising. After more than an hour in the truck, I located only two sets of tracks, two yearlings traveling together through a dense stand of jack pine. Had there been a buck track, I'd have taken it. But no such luck this time.

Itching to get in the woods and get my boots on the ground, I decided to head down to Muzzleloader Mountain for a mid-day stalking session. Approaching from the east, I made my way around, then uphill into the wind. Nearing the top, I bumped a pair of does out of a tall stand of hemlocks. Whoops. Too fast, you fool. I stopped to look around. Too late. The deer had already bolted and headed west, then south around the hill.

Continuing my climb with a little more care now, I sneaked and peeked my way toward the top. Along the way, I passed the old pine stump that bore my initials at the scene of my 2012 muzzleloader hunt.

A few more steps and I emerged at the cliff-side precipice. I took in the sight of the canyon and the thunderous sound of the waterfalls below. Every time I walk that cliff-top trail, I'm mesmerized by the beauty.

Completing my hunt, I made my way into the collection of small outcrops and peaks scattered around the top of the mountain. With little fresh deer sign and a dearth of acorns on this particular hill, I had mostly given up on the hunt and was thinking about making my way down the mountain.

THE LEGEND OF THUNDER CANYON

As I rounded a ten-foot rock outcrop, I looked up and into the eyes of a doe, less than twenty yards away. As surprised as I was, she instantly bolted and was accompanied by her fawn in a panicked ascent off the southwest slope. Good thing there wasn't a buck there, or I would've blown it yet again. I had lost my concentration and was moving way too fast and not looking where I was going, both common and easy mistakes to make while still-hunting. In this game, anything less than perfection can lead to instant and complete failure.

For the afternoon hunt, I left the gun at home and decided to take on a new hunting partner, my pound hound, Cajun. Actually, we were just headed out for the daily walk. But this time we went for several hours and delved deep into deer country. After Cajun's skunk experience in July, we've kept him on the leash, walking at all times connected to his person via chest harness and strap, and this day was no different.

It's nice being connected to the back of a strong dog when you have to climb a hill. Conversely, it's not so nice being attached to a dog pulling downhill, or when the dog encounters a hot chipmunk scent. But Cajun did pretty good. He was excited and seemed to understand my explanation of the adventure at hand.

We walked a couple of miles along the oak plateau, occasionally working to the edge of the ridge and peeking out over the winding creek bottom below. Nearing the far northwest end of the plateau, Cajun stopped and sniffed the air, looking into the wind. I paused with him and, seeing nothing, urged him forward. Two steps further, we froze as several deer broke cover about sixty yards to the north and bounded away. If only I had listened to him when he pointed, we might not have spooked them. Good boy, Cajun.

Getting later in the day, we turned and slowly set out to make our way home. Pausing several times at likely crossings, we sat together for fifteen to thirty minutes at a time, silently watching and listening. I was surprised by the canine's penchant for sitting quiet and still. Likewise, I was impressed by his sensory awareness and curiosity, tuning in to study every sound, smell, and movement in the woods. Further along the trail, I paused at another place where I expected deer to cross.

We waited just a few minutes, then proceeded again. Proceeded, that is, to spook another deer, this one a single deer who was traveling a scrape line along the rim of the canyon. I couldn't tell what it was, but I was bummed to mess up another chance at perhaps seeing a buck. Once again, if only I had waited a little longer or gone a little slower, I might not have blown it.

Still making our way home, as we neared a trail intersection at the heart of the plateau, Cajun came to an abrupt pointing halt, searching with his nose to the air. After a brief pause, I saw nothing, and urged the dog onward.

Cajun, the pound hound. A proud and patient hunting partner.

Thooom, ta thoom, ta thoom, da doomp, da doomp. A group of at least five deer broke out of the oak and balsam thicket, just forty yards ahead and scattered to all points south. Cajun lunged forward, rising up on his hind legs, straining against his leash. The excited canine then let out a little howl, not unlike a baby blood hound trembling at the feet of a treed coon.

I pulled him back to earth and sought to settle his enthusiasm. Boy, does he have a good nose. Twice now, he'd seen the deer with his nose and told me, long before we could see them with our eyes.

Perhaps we'll do this again some day. It was fun goin' deer huntin' with my little buddy. Fun for him too, I could tell. We made our way home and by the end of the day, I'd seen more deer than in any other day all year. Plus I got to enjoy a day in the woods with my best friend. It was a good day.
---Daily total: 16 deer, 0 bucks. Season total: 56 deer, 0 bucks

13 END OF THE LINE

December 12

As I stepped into the ninth day of the muzzleloader season, it was getting down to the wire, with just two more days to hunt. If I was gonna do it, I had better do it soon. It was time to make hay or get out of the way. After dragging myself from the comfort of my sleeping nest, once again I was on the road at around 6:30 a.m.

Unfortunately, by this point, having carved a full twenty pounds from my already lean physique, I knew I no longer had the strength to quietly climb a single mountain. My legs were blown out to the point where I struggled to carry my 163-pound bag of bones up a simple half-flight of stairs. I knew it would be days before I could regain my strength, and I was out of time, almost out of options. Already exhausted by the miles of hiking day after day after day, I made the conscious decision to compromise my values.

Rather than continue my marathon of taking the fight to the adversary, I decided to take the passive approach and employ the ambush technique. If I couldn't catch up with my quarry, I'd just have to wait for him to come to me. While sitting for extended periods isn't something I normally do, considering the woods and weather conditions combined with my extreme physical fatigue, I really had no other viable options. I wasn't staying home, and I really didn't want to drive around in the truck all day.

So I made my way to the tent blind I'd set up at the northeast rim of Thunder Canyon. I sat there a few days ago and saw nothing, yet my hopes were still high. I'd seen fresh buck sign there on my last few visits, so I knew a buck was still using the area. As I made my way down the trail, I was moved by the anticipation, confident this might finally be *the* day. Zipping myself in the tent well before daylight, with a fresh dusting of snow it was looking like a good morning for a hunt. Gradually, after seeing only bluejays, as the hours crept by my confidence slowly eroded.

At 9:30, I called the wife on the cellphone, hoping to get an update on the weather report. As she reported temperatures forecast to climb to thirty-

65

eight degrees by noon along with a twenty percent chance of drizzle, the wheels in my mind started to turn. We talked for almost thirty minutes, happy to finally be spending time together after my extended stay in the woods. She wished me well and I thanked her. Immediately, I was thinking about the possibilities of taking one more track, or maybe just one more climb up the mountain. With a dusting of snow setting to melt and drizzle on the way, I thought, just maybe. Maybe I can give it one more go. It would likely be my last chance for the year to make a good sneak hunt. The forecast for the next day was guaranteeing an all-day soaking rain, so this was it. Tomorrow, I thought, will be the day to sit all day in a tent.

Even though I was confident a deer might show up here if I waited long enough, my mind was already made up. Like a magnet being drawn to metal, I couldn't resist the pull. I had to go. I packed up my bags and got ready to set out, one more time, for Thirty-Point Mountain.

At 10 o'clock, standing in the blind, fully ready to go, I take one more look around. I look to the east and see movement. It's a deer! Walking steadily up the oak ridge, it's heading right for me. Emerging from behind some small pines, he comes into full view at forty yards. It's a buck!

Immediately, my weapon is up, ready to go. I set, take careful aim, and squeeze the trigger. Right away, I know it's a good shot. Not great, but I'm certain it will be good enough. He's no trophy buck, but he's a buck and I got him. I record a few minutes of video, shoot a few photos, then pause to savor the moment.

At 10:10, I called Dawn again, this time to tell her that the good luck she'd sent really worked. I told her I had just gotten off the phone, and five minutes later, here he comes. After talking for a few minutes and sharing my story, I got back to the task at hand and took the time to record the moment in my field notes.

It was perhaps the best hunt of the black-powder season. My scouting led me to him. I found his spot, his active scrape line, and set my spot. It worked perfectly. My second morning here, and it's a successful hunt. Who cares that he was only a spike-horn and that my chosen weapon was the camera. The hunt worked as planned, the buck lived to grow another year older, nobody got hurt, and everybody walks away happy.

Now that's what I call a good hunt. I finally got him. After 24 straight days of hunting, on the penultimate day of the season, I finally had a good clear shot opportunity at a buck.

A few minutes after he arrived, he caught my wind and silently snuck away. Likewise, after a few minutes, I silently retreated and set off on my next adventure.

Two days left in the season and finally, here comes a deer. It's a buck.

By 11, I was on my way up Thirty-Point Mountain for that one last sneak-hunt of the year. At noon I was back at the scene of my first encounter with the Legend and ready to settle in for the rest of the day. As I waited in my hiding spot among the oaks, I listened intently, watching all around for any sign of animate life.

Not seeing much, I was in a reflective state. Staring at the scene of my epic failure, knowing I would forever be haunted by my memories on this mountain, my mind raced. I pulled out the journal to capture my feelings.

Ah, the agony of going back and reliving my failed moment. I tried to see the success in getting myself into that moment of opportunity. But try as I might, I can't help but think of the split second and the inches that separated me from the ultimate success.

Until the last light faded from the sky, I held my vigil on the mountaintop. My reward never arrived, and I saw nary a deer that evening. What I did see, over and over in my mind's eye, was an image of the biggest buck I'd ever seen in the big woods, a split second of sight seared into my brain.

Funny how a split second can stay stuck in the mind for so long. I ached to take a good long look at the Legend, to see just exactly what he looked like. Instead, I was left grasping at a spilt-second glimpse of an image straight out of my dreams. The memory was almost surreal. Like seeing a ghost. Vivid yet vague. Clear and foggy. Real and unreal.

---Daily total: 1 deer, 1 buck. Season total: 57 deer, 1 buck

December 13

On the tenth and last day of the 2015 Upper Peninsula muzzleloader deer season, for the final time I was up and at 'em well before first light. With a forecast of rain coming to fruition, my last stand was planned to be made in the tent blind on the canyon rim. For once, I genuinely looked forward to setting out to sit in one spot for ten straight hours. With a driving rain well under way as I drove through the dark, I was pretty sure I had the best option for sitting through a soaker of a day.

After getting zipped into the dry blind, I made myself cozy in my favorite wooden chair. If nothing else, I was going to be comfortable. Armed with both a wool and a down blanket, a hearty lunch, two bottles of water, and reading and writing materials, I was ready for the day. To help pass the time, to help fight off drowsiness and for my listening enjoyment, I also brought along my iPod loaded with my favorite music along with the radio so I could tune in to the Packers and Lions games. It was going to be a good day, rain and all. At least I wouldn't get bored.

By 7:40 I was settled in, well before shooting light, which arrived at about 8:15. At 8:40, I had two deer come down from the north. Making their way through the oak valley, they slowly worked their way onto the oak ridge in front of me. Through the rain on the dark and dreary morning, I couldn't tell, that second one, if it was a buck or doe. As they emerged into the clearing before me, my excitement was snuffed when I saw they were both young-uns. They hung around and ate for awhile before being spooked by the sound of my camera and bounding back to the north. Buck or not, it was nice to see a couple of deer and get the skunk out of the boat.

By 9, the animal activity in the woods grew quiet as the din of the rain rose to an almost pounding sound. It wasn't quite cats and dogs, but it was almost raining frogs. With an all-day rain ahead, I didn't expect to see much more life. No matter. It was nice to be sitting high and dry on a watery day in the woods.

An hour passed, then two, then three and four. Then 2 o'clock came and went, followed by 3, then 4. After the conclusion of the Lions game, I tuned in to Wayne and Larry for the Packers broadcast. It was actually surprising how quickly the time seemed to be rolling away. I suppose, like when having fun, time can fly when you're comfortable. And cozy I was, watching the rain come down, nestled under blankets of feather and fur. Even without seeing deer, boredom never came calling. Soon it was prime time and the rain started to relent.

By 5 p.m., time was running out, yet I held out hope. At 5:15, darkness was settling in and the shapes of the forest were starting to merge into the night. I scanned the view, looking to the north, the west, and then to the south.

That looks different, I thought. Peering into the twilight, looking south into the canyon, something looked a little out of place. All along, I'd been expecting a big buck to come up from the south and out of the canyon, yet that was the one direction in which I'd yet to see a deer. Staring south at the suspicious shape, after a few moments, the shape moved.

It's a deer. Incoming.

While it's clearly a full-size deer, the failing light delays positive gender identification. After first seeing the deer at about eighty yards, within seconds the deer approaches to fifty yards then disappears behind the belly of the ridge. A moment later he reappears just thirty yards below me, eating acorns from the forest floor.

He raises his head. It's a buck! Sure is. No doubt. In the fading light, I could clearly see brow tines rising several inches above his forehead. Watching over the gun sights, I strain to see more. He grabs more nuts, then raises his head and looks around. There's nothing more to see. It's that same spike-horn who showed up the previous morning.

Good to see you, little fella. Good to see you again.

Within minutes, the last light of the season faded away. I looked on as the animated shapes before me slowly faded into the surroundings of the dark forest. And with that, it was over. Another season in the books.

Left to savor the fading sight of a buck that lived on in the moments after the season ended, all I could really think about was the Legend of Thunder Canyon. It was a season to remember, all right. Try as I might, I knew I could never forget about my memories on the mountain. I would forever be haunted by my moments of failure in the presence of a ghost.

---Daily total: 5 deer, 1 buck. Season total: 62 deer, 2 bucks

****

2015 Muzzleloader Season Stats:

62 deer sightings, 2 from road.
2 buck sightings, 0 from road.
10 days hunted = 6.2 deer/day
88 hours hunted = 1 deer per 1.42 hours
1 buck per 5 days = 1 buck per 44 hours hunted.

****

14 IN RETROSPECT

Sitting in my blind on that rainy last day of the season, I had plenty of downtime to consider my year of hunting. I pulled out my field notes one last time and, looking back on my adventures, I took a moment to jot down some reflections on the season. The most vivid recollection that stuck out was the evening of my great failure.

I was the Detroit Lions, Chicago Cubs, Cincinnati Bengals and Cleveland Browns, all wrapped up into one putrid ball of failure. To a degree that few others before had stooped, I inexplicably snatched defeat from the jaws of the ultimate victory. On the biggest stage, a split second and a couple of inches separated me from success in my 25-year quest.

Still frustrated with my multiple failures during the season, I made more notes on key points to remember. Expounding in the voice of No Shillings Sherlock, it was all familiar information, from the book of "I Should've Known Better." Maybe if I write out the obvious, perhaps the information will resonate.

All of the best equipment in the world can't make up for bad decisions and poor hunting technique. Proper technique and sound decision making will get you through those critical last few inches in the most critical fraction of a second. A little good luck helps too. Hard work and good luck isn't enough. It takes sound fundamentals and good decision making at key moments.

You can't catch a deer physically. You can't out-run him and you can't out-walk him either. Instead, you have to out-think him, out-smart him, or simply hang around where he goes and wait for him.

You can't sneak up on him in the wrong conditions: dry, still, sunny, crunchy. But you can sneak up on him in the right conditions: wet, snowy, windy, drippy. Either way, you have to go slow, think about it, and wait for it. The patient man survives.

After walking many miles on the road to success, I fell one step short of reaching the top.

And the season came to a close. Exhilarating, exhausting, and excruciating, it was an experience like no other. Never had I worked so hard, walked so many miles, dedicated so much time to a season's hunt. I'd done all I could do, given everything I had, and in the end, I'd lost the game. Reality setting in, it was a bitter nut to crunch. I had my chances. But in the moment of truth, I fell short and my opponent emerged as the victor.

15 POSTSEASON ANALYSIS

In the week following the conclusion of the deer season, I was consumed with the split-second image of the Legend, seared into my brain like the brand on a bull's butt. It was a feeling that just wouldn't go away. I could see it clearly, and yet the image was foggy. Wanting nothing more than to have a picture to replace the flash in my mind's eye, I made a plan for one more hunt.

On Sunday, December 20, I returned to a snowy Thirty-Point Mountain, armed this time with a trail camera, corn, and sugar beets. I was bound and determined to get him, one way or another. Upon arrival atop the ridge, I found the area under the oaks completely torn up. It was as if the whole herd had gathered on this one hilltop then stayed for days, trampling down the entire area. Among the tracks was one good buck track along with his bed, situated with a commanding view in the middle of the meadow. The owner of this hill had obviously been here just yesterday. I was confident I would get him this time and left the camera with high hopes.

After a week, with a big snowstorm on the way, I decided to retrieve the camera. The area was thick with deer tracks, and the food I left long since gone. I pulled the camera and said goodbye to the mountain. Until next year. Walking the mile through the dark woods and back to the truck, I could hardly wait to see the photos.

Not able to wait for the drive home, after arriving at the truck I pulled the memory card from the trail cam and placed it in my pocket camera for a quick peek. There were some photos all right, more than 2,400 in all. It was a good spot for the camera trap, and the deer fell into it promptly. Day after day, doe after doe came and went, pausing to munch at the treats I had left.

On the sixth day of the trap set, I finally got what I was looking for: a buck. He had come in at night, stayed for a few minutes, then moved on. An hour later he returned, this time staying for forty minutes. Later in the night, he returned, only to leave and return again, just before first light.

CAMERA 2   27 DEC 2015 02:50 am

A young buck at the all-night buffet. Could it be the Legend of the future?

The next night he had come back once more, and that was the last I saw of him. Unfortunately, he wasn't the curly-tops I was looking for. Instead, he was merely a fat spike-horn with big feet to grow into. In the course of one week and among more than 2,000 photos, he was the only buck photographed. Perhaps in another three or four years, he can take the throne as the next Legend of Thunder Canyon.

Meanwhile, all I had to look at of my encounter with the current Legend was a split-second flash of memory, played back over and over in my mind. It would be understated to say I was disappointed that I didn't get a photo of the Legend.

A Side Note, for Perspective

With the unusually mild weather of December 2015, for the first time in twenty years, we traveled to Lower Michigan to visit with family for the holidays. Not ready to accept complete defeat for the season, I jumped at the opportunity to spend a few more days deer hunting.

This time I would be hunting with the bow and arrow on some of the finest deer hunting land in Michigan. It was a place full of hunting history, the old family farm in Jackson County. And while it was late in the season, I was certain I would see some deer.

My farm hunt started on December 25, and by 8:15 that morning, I had already seen a coyote and three deer, including a big six-point, all of which passed by under my tree stand, less than twenty yards away. The deer continued to come and go throughout my hunts over the next three days. With critter sightings including coyotes, cranes, deer, ducks, geese, rabbits, songbirds, and squirrels, it was a wildlife wonderland. By December 27, after five hunts over three days, I had seen a total of forty-eight deer including six bucks.

For a little perspective, we compare the results of a few days hunting in the farmlands of southern Michigan to the results of a whole season spent hunting in the big woods up north. In three days of easy hunting in southern Michigan, I saw nearly as many deer and more bucks than I saw in an entire season of hard hunting in the U.P.

To me, it's interesting to compare my statistics for the respective seasons side by side. You can see from the stats, hunting deer in the big woods is a vastly different challenge than hunting deer in the farmlands. What really stands out is the number of buck sightings per hour hunted.

Of course, hunting is rarely easy, even in farm country. And while I could've taken several of the bucks I saw on the farm had I been hunting with a firearm, this time I was bowhunting and camera hunting. As it turned out, the opponents claimed victory again, as none of the bucks I saw offered a good shot opportunity for either weapon.

Seeing a big buck and getting a good shot opportunity can be two entirely different things.

****

2015 Deer Hunting Statistics

Sixteen-day U.P. Firearm Season Stats:

42 deer sightings, 16 from road.
3 buck sightings, 1 from road.
14.5 days hunted = 2.89 deer/day
145 hours hunted = 1 deer per 3.46 hours
1 buck per 4.83 days = 1 buck per 48.3 hours hunted.

Ten-day U.P. Muzzleloader Season Stats:

62 deer sightings, 2 from road.
2 buck sightings, 0 from road.
10 days hunted = 6.2 deer/day
88 hours hunted = 1 deer per 1.42 hours
1 buck per 5 days = 1 buck per 44 hours hunted.

Three-day Lower Michigan Archery Hunt Stats:

48 deer sightings, 0 from road.
6 buck sightings, 0 from road.
3 days hunted = 16 deer/day
15 hours hunted = 3.2 deer per hour
2 bucks per day = 1 buck per 2.5 hours hunted.

****

16 THE REST OF THE STORY

Into the last days of December now, and with the season over, I still couldn't shake the image of the Legend from my mind. For that matter, I'll probably never flush that image from my mind, the biggest buck I ever saw in the big woods, looking me in the eye at thirty yards.

Still thinking about that buck, I took a drive up to his turf hoping to see some sign of his survival. A simple track in the snow was the best I was hoping for. Along the way, I ran into my old friend Joe, and we stopped to talk. I asked Joe about his and his boys' seasons. Like myself, they had ended the season without putting up any venison.

Then I went out on the limb. Knowing that Joe's camp was only a couple of miles from Thirty-Point Mountain, I took the calculated risk of sharing my story. While I risked revealing my top secret, I thought it was safe to share the secret with Joe. Old Joe, who happens to be the dad of my good friend Little Joe, is a man you can trust. Besides, I thought, chances are, Old Joe probably already knew about the Legend. A buck like that doesn't go unnoticed. In calculating the risk, I knew that the potential reward of revealing my secret might be an actual photo of the Legend. It was my last and only hope to get a good long look at the Legend of Thunder Canyon.

With measured enthusiasm, I told my tale of blowing my chance at a pretty good buck, not too far from Joe's camp. When he asked how good of a buck, I tried to low-key it, not wanting to reveal too much unnecessarily.

"Oh, he was a good one," I said as I held my hands spread wide, "the biggest buck I ever saw around here, he was at least eighteen inches wide."

Joe chuckled a bit. "Eighteen inches, eh? Your hands are showing about twenty-one inches."

"Well, he could very well have been 20 inches," I replied. "I didn't have much time to look. All I know is he was the biggest, widest buck I ever saw. I don't want to exaggerate, and if I said twenty inches, people might doubt me. You guys didn't happen to get a picture of him, did you?"

"How much money you got?" Joe shot back with a laugh.

"I'd give twenty bucks for his picture, right now," I said, fully serious.

Joe pulled his phone from his pocket. "Yeah, we saw him all right. We call him Bullwinkle. He showed up in late October, then disappeared later in November." He scrolled through the camera.

"When did you see him last?" I inquired.

"Well, just last week, right around Christmas, he was back. But he only comes in at night." Arriving at the correct photo, he handed me the phone.

"That's him!" I exclaimed. That's the guy. Wow! What a monster." The phone's screen showed a clear photo of an exceptionally wide-racked buck. Big by any hunter's standards, the buck sported antlers that shot straight out and around, extending several inches beyond the tips of the ears on each side. It looked almost surreal. With a solid ten points and tines extending up eight inches or more, it was a magnificent buck for the big woods of the U.P.

I reached for my wallet and pulled a bill, offering it up in exchange for a printed photo. As much as I had thought about that buck, I would've happily paid some cash for one little picture.

But Old Joe didn't want my money. Instead, and to my delight, Joe kindly offered to email the photo my way. I gave him my address and thanked him over and over for sharing.

The Legend of Thunder Canyon, caught on Old Joe's trail camera in October 2015.
(Photo by Old Joe)

Fortunately for me, my friends the Joes are a lot like my dad and brothers, like Mike, Marv, Paul, Scott, Tim, Tom, the Johns, and the few other hunting friends I have in the area; they're as good of people as you can find anywhere. Hard-working, honest, friendly, fun people. A lot like most Yoopers, actually. They're just plain good people: helpful, generous, old-fashioned, good folks. It's the Yooper way.

It was a kind gesture to share the photo, as Joe could have kept *his* knowledge of the Legend a secret to himself. I thanked him again.

Little did he know, but he'd made my day. Made my season, really. Finally, I had something to look at to confirm the vision of the ghost in my mind. Finally some closure that I could live with. And with that, my hunting season officially concluded.

The Legend, as seen at Old Joe's Buffet in mid-November.   (Photo by Old Joe)

17 LOOKING BACK, LOOKING FORWARD

Now a couple of months removed from the season, my wounds have begun to heal as the pain and agony of defeat have begun to subside. I'll admit, I'm not quite over the whole thing, but I'm coming to terms with it now. Even in defeat, I've come to appreciate the opportunity I had to face off with the Legend.

Win or lose, to have ascended to compete with the highest level of competition in my chosen field, I'm proud to have made it to the big show. I gave it my all and competed with great honor and integrity. I left it all on the field, did all I could do, and in the end, I congratulate my opponent. He was as lucky as he was smart, but it's no accident that he prevailed. We had a heck of a battle, and he deserved to win as much as I did.

Perhaps it's best this way. In many ways, I feel better having lost and knowing he's alive than I would've felt, having won and knowing that I'd ended his life. After enduring all the dangers the Legend has endured, it almost seems he's more deserving of keeping his life than I was of taking it. And besides, had it ended any differently for the Legend, I wouldn't have had the opportunity to experience one of the greatest stories of my life.

Moving into the new year, with snow filling the forest, the hunters have returned to their lives, far away from the woods. Meanwhile, the creatures of the forest have gone back to living in harmony and maintaining their natural balance in the big woods. And deep in those woods, in the mountains surrounding Thunder Canyon, the Legend lives on.

As for me, I continue to have nightmares about my epic failure. In my waking hours, I often find my mind wandering back to the events of my quest, recalling lessons learned and scheming plans for next time.

While I fell flat on my face just short of the finish line this year, I've already set my sights on a return to the game for next year. I know it'll be tougher next year, as my body ages and continues to rust. And I know, someday there won't be a next year.

But for now, my quest continues. And as I rise from my seat at the desk to throw another log on the fire, I'll make my way around the house on tiptoes, already in training for my next encounter with the Legend of Thunder Canyon.

The Legend of Thunder Canyon, as seen leaving Old Joe's and still going strong near the end of another hunting season   (Photo by Old Joe)

THE LEGEND OF THUNDER CANYON

DUANE PAPE

Part II

18 A NEW YEAR ARRIVES

I suppose I wasn't much different from any of the other hunters out there. We all dream of the day when we finally get the chance to tag our buck of a lifetime. While I was lucky enough to experience that day in my second year of hunting, I still had a lifetime of hunting ahead of me.

And though I had already tagged the buck of every hunter's dreams, I still yearned to someday get a monster buck in the big woods. Having hunted in the Upper Peninsula for more than twenty years, however, I knew the odds of even seeing a huge buck in these big woods were pretty slim.

Then I had my chance of a lifetime. And I blew it. Twice. But in blowing it, I learned the dream could possibly come true. With that, my yearning grew. Perhaps it was my past failure that drove my hunger for the future.

Stepping into the new year of 2016, my thoughts remained filled with images of the Legend of Thunder Canyon. Having already written my story, I was moving forward, moving on from that season of 2015. Yet, try as I might, I still couldn't flush the image of that great buck from my mind.

By April, spring was on the way and I found myself daydreaming and scheming plans for my next move. While I feared the Legend had failed to make it through the winter, I maintained hope that he might have survived. With that hope, I couldn't wait to get out scouting in the spring to look for his shed antlers.

As mid-April rolled around, the big melt was on its way. Then it hit. The big one. It was April 14, and I had just finished the taxes. That night, I went for groceries to make the food that would fuel my next week of adventures. Eager to get on with the annual spring rituals, I hurriedly carried way too many groceries down to the house, then up the stairs. Dropping the load in the kitchen, as I bent to set the stuff on the floor, I felt a sharp pain in my lower back. I tried to straighten up, but my back had other ideas. The intense pain dropped me to my knees.

Right away, I knew I was in trouble. Holding the counter, I pulled myself to my feet and was greeted by a great pain. Dammit. I should've stretched out. Though I knew it was probably too late, I desperately tried to bend this way and that to work out the kink. With no such luck in the moment, I went to bed hoping for better luck in the morning.

By morning, the pain was crippling. Not only could I not sit up, I couldn't even lift my legs off the bed. I rolled out of the sack and crookedly made my way into the day. For breakfast, I could neither sit nor stand, so I sort of hunched over, leaning into the counter for support. For my tooth brushing, my only option was to kneel in front of the sink. It was the worst pain I ever felt in my back, and that's after a lifetime of back pain.

It was done. Before it even started, my highly anticipated springtime season of adventure was over. There would be no trout fishing, no shed hunting, no agate hunting, and no golf. For two grueling weeks, it was all I could do just to survive. Like the hunchback, I hobbled around, longing to have the ability to get out and do what I do. It was tough to simply eat and even tougher to sleep.

At the end of April I couldn't take it anymore. My back wasn't getting better, and all I could think about was finding those shed antlers. The only thing that seemed to ease the suffering was going for a walk. Now, I was in no shape for a big hike, but I couldn't resist the calling of the Legend. So at the end of the month, I took my trusty walking stick for a good hike.

Up into the hills I went, hiking the ridges where I first met the Legend, searching under the numerous oaks for his obsolete bones of yesteryear. After the oaks, I made my way up a mountain, down and around through a canyon, then back through the pine thickets in between, hoping to stumble upon a miracle.

Like an old dog who remains young at heart, I pushed too far and paid the price. The pain at times was intolerable, often dropping me to the ground, where I would find some awkward position to temporarily ease the excruciating burden. After a few miles of hiking and hurting, I could barely go on. Driven only by my hunger for food and thirst for shelter, I eventually found the strength to hobble my way home. I never found an antler that day, and I never got back to look again.

What I did find that day was another grim reminder of my season of failure. Hobbling along the old skid road, heading up onto the ridge where I missed the Legend the second time, there in the path next to a pile of coyote scat lay a tattered old red bandana. I poked my walking stick into the rag and scooped it up for a closer look. It was a foreign sight to see in these deep woods, yet it sort of looked familiar. With the center of the bandana completely eaten away, all that remained was the frayed outer edge of the handkerchief. Then it occurred to me what exactly I was looking at.

My old red bandana, lost in 2015, found and chewed by coyotes, then left for the buzzards.

Located less than 100 yards from where I'd missed the Legend and subsequently sliced open my forehead, here lay my old red snot-rag, the same one I used last year to wipe away the blood from my brow. I took it off the stick, shook it off, and put in my pocket. Obviously, some coyote had found it where I unknowingly dropped it, chewed out the portion containing my blood, then left the remainder for the buzzards. It was an ironic twist to the tale, an unexpected relic found at the scene of my great train wreck of a deer hunt. While it was a soiled souvenir from the big game lost, it was a treasure to me nonetheless. Serving as a reminder of what might have been, I carried it forward as a talisman with hopes for what it might bring in the future.

Similar to the hairs of the Legend that I found on his licking branches and proceeded to chew on, I would carry this unique piece of my story on future hunts with the hope it might carry some good luck. Perhaps after sitting out there for the winter and into the spring, maybe all the bad luck it might have carried had been washed away.

The other thing I saw that day was a group of three big deer, including one that was significantly larger than its peers. In the barren woods of early spring, less than a half mile from the location where I first met the Legend, it looked like a bachelor group of deer. Could it have been the Legend? I had a strange feeling it might have been. I hobbled home filled with hope.

After pushing way too far on a bad back, I was forced to spend the next two weeks convalescing at home. By the time I was able to go for another decent walk, the bug season was on, vegetation was emerging, and the shed hunting season was over. At least I got the chance to look once.

For all I knew, those antlers could be anywhere, for miles and miles. Perhaps they weren't meant to be mine. Besides, I didn't really want to spend too much time stomping around in the Legend's home turf. If he was still alive, the last thing I wanted to do was scare him off into another territory. Reluctantly, I had no choice but to leave his castaway antlers for the rodents.

19 COMPLETING THE BOOK

By the beginning of the summer of 2016, I had completed a couple rounds of edits on the book and I put it on the shelf to age for a while. After having thought about that deer every day for months now, I tried to put it out of my mind. Yet the images of my great misadventure lingered. I had still not shared the story with my brothers and looked forward to doing so.

When school resumed in the fall, I dusted off the manuscript and got back to work. Diligently, I plugged in all the corrections and improvements I had previously identified. At the end of the third round of edits, I printed up a copy and gave it a read. It was a masterpiece. A classic for the ages.

I told Dawn my thoughts about the book and supported my claim with the most interesting aspect of this hunting tale: It's a story about a hunt, and this time the deer won. I couldn't have been more proud of my telling of the tale of my failure. Because it was so much more than a simple tale of failure. It was a true story about a pure and riveting adventure. The fact is, in the end, for once, both the deer and the hunter won. The deer because he survived. The hunter because he had the opportunity to participate in one of the greatest hunts of all time.

As is often the case, the hunting season approached quickly, and before I knew it November had arrived. For the first weekend of the month, I traveled to southern Michigan to spend some time camera hunting on the family farm with Dad. It turned out to be a great weekend with lots of critters sighted and a few nice photos the result. The best part was the quality time shared in the field with Dad. In the thirty-third renewal of our annual hunting tradition, we talked and laughed and recalled highlights of years gone by, indeed some of the greatest days of our lives.

At the end of the weekend I delivered copies of the book to my dad and brothers. I couldn't wait for their feedback, and I didn't have to wait long.

Within days, I heard from my brothers and the reviews were consistently positive. Brother Ray was the first to call and, in his voice, I could hear a genuine and pulsating excitement. *Awesome* was one word I heard, *compelling* another.

Brother Brian suggested that perhaps I was being too hard on myself.

What he couldn't know was what I had learned: In order to get that buck, I would have to work harder than I'd ever worked and my execution would have to be flawless. Like an athlete striving for a championship, the relentless pursuit of perfection was the only way to achieve a flawless performance. And in order to conquer the greatest of foes, a perfect performance is often prerequisite. If I was going to win, I had to hold myself to the highest standard. No room for candy coatings or good enough. Each day I had to find a way to be better. In order to do so, I had to take a hard look at myself, to find and fix my flaws. In fact, I really needed to be harder on myself if I wanted to win the championship.

Overall, and to my delight, both of the readers found the story to be entertaining and fun. As hoped, my audience reported the feeling of having been delivered to the scenes I had so carefully illustrated. Perhaps the most telling piece of feedback was the fact that both of my intended readers had consumed the entire book in one sitting.

Now granted, my seventy-seven-page story was no encyclopedia, but the fact is, the readers found the piece so compelling, they literally couldn't put it down. My mission accomplished, I could finally put the story to rest. Regardless of anything else that may come of the book, I had achieved my goal in successfully telling my story by way of text. At least now they could have a little better understanding of what I do and why I do it.

Meanwhile, deep down, I had the feeling I'd created a masterpiece. As it stood, I thought it was one of the greatest deer hunting tales ever told. While the project was a long way from completion, I'd come to believe the book was worth publishing and it would be well received. Upon completion of the peer review, my suspicions were bolstered.

And as the process proceeded, my efforts created a transformative experience, for in failure, I had found success. But the next steps of manufacturing the masterpiece would have to wait for now. With the arrival of November, once again, it was time for me to go out and continue living the story of my life.

20 CONTAGIOUS ENTHUSIASM

One of the things that came with sharing Part I of the book was a reciprocated shared interest in the saga I was engaged in. While speaking with my brother Ray, I was moved by his excitement for my opportunity to single out and hunt the same deer for a number of years. I felt like he was more excited for the opportunity to resume the battle than I was. Maybe that's because I knew how difficult the journey had already been, or perhaps because I had already calculated the long odds against ever seeing the Legend again.

While talking with my dad during our early November archery and camera hunt, he too was eager to discuss the next chapter in the story of the Legend. Dad suggested something like: "Maybe you can write the next part of the book this year, as you go after the Legend one more time."

"Yeah, maybe," I replied. Or maybe not. In reality, the story might already be over. It's fun to imagine there could be one more chapter, but the fact is, the chances of ever seeing that particular deer again are extremely slim. Even if he survived the winter, he's one little critter in a big, big woods. The odds of seeing him again would be similar to the odds of lightning striking thrice in the same place.

Despite my realistic outlook, the image of the Legend continued to burn in my mind. While I was carrying my bow and arrows during the archery season, deep down I knew there was no chance I would be shooting at a deer with the bow. From the start, for me, it was a camera-hunt only. With the firearm season fast approaching, I had way too many things to accomplish in order to be ready for my potential date with the Legend. With just over a week before the gun season, there was no time for tagging and processing any other deer.

November 1, 2016. It was an easy decision to shoot this eight-point with only the camera.

Later in the weekend, Dad invited me for a hunt on the farm during the firearm season. As much as I enjoyed our camera hunt together and looked forward to another, I had to decline. Despite the promising sightings we had on the farm, I explained that I was sort of pigeonholed. Having carried on the hunt for the Legend to this point and having written the book, I really had no choice but to go all out in this year's hunt for the Legend. And besides, deep down, there was really only one deer that I was interested in hunting.

Drawing closer to the 2016 firearm season, as I talked about the book with a couple of friends who'd read it, I was inspired by their belief that I'd get that buck. It almost felt like they had more belief in me than I did. Perhaps that's because only I knew the true reality of the immense challenge. Even after having read the details of my odyssey, they could not conceive of the difficulty in the task that lay ahead.

I tried to deflect the enthusiasm with my armor of reality, a shield against high expectation and the potential for disappointment. In all of my conversations on the topic, I made a concerted effort to temper the enthusiasm. In conclusion, I always remarked that it is already one of the greatest stories ever told, and if it's already over, I'm okay with that. It really was an honor and a thrill just to be a part of it to this point, win or lose. As it was, one of my favorite aspects of the story was that, in the end, the deer lived to see another day. And if that really was the end of the story, that really was okay.

Yet the enthusiasm of my family and friends was contagious, and soon, I too was growing optimistic about the season to come. As the season drew nearer, each time we discussed the topic, I would always conclude my side of the story by proclaiming my belief that, regardless of the outcome, I *would* cross paths with the Legend again. I'd become a believer, and the belief of my people bolstered my resolve.

21 PREPARING FOR THE CHALLENGE

My 2016 renewal in the battle with the Legend began long before the season rolled around. Aside from my literary pursuits in reliving and telling the story, my quest for the Legend was in the back of my mind every day.

The physical training began in June as my sore old back relented just enough so I could begin my daily training hikes. Leashed to the back of our seventy-five-pound hound dog, every day we made our way through the backyard hills, up and down and around through the forest. Our original loop of 1.1 miles wasn't quite enough so I expanded the trail to 1.4 miles, then expanded again to a 1.7-mile route. From start to finish, the trails winding through the oak and hemlock forest climb and descend more than 200 feet in elevation.

And because our pound hound is, in fact, a hound, he has this unique biological feature that seemingly renders his ears completely useless when his nose is engaged. And since he really loves to chomp chipmunks, chase deer, and corner skunks, we loving and responsible fur-baby parents now find the need to find ourselves always attached to this pull-happy puppy. Now, that's not such a bad thing when going up-hill. But on those damp and dank days when all the smells of the forest are lingering just above the ground, the task of holding back a huffing hound is a bit like fighting a monstrous four-legged fish. The whole time you're walking forward, you have to be pulling hard backward. It's a strength-building core workout like no other, like walking upstream in a strong flow of chest-deep water.

Near the end of the summer I begin the annual wood-gathering ritual. In order to heat the house through a six- to seven-month month Upper Peninsula winter, a fella needs a good amount of wood. In my case, it generally takes at least ten full-size truckloads of maple and oak to get us through. And when I say a truckload of wood, I mean logs of eight to twelve feet in length and as big around as my leg. A full load fills the Silverado bed from side to side, bottom to top, with logs protruding two to four feet beyond the back of the tailgate.

Of course, all of those trees need to be felled, chopped to haul length, bucked out to the road, loaded into the truck, then unloaded onto the backyard woodpile. The actual chopping of the logs to burnable lengths comes later. As you might imagine, the wood-making process serves as the foundation of my seasonal upper-body strength training. And I can assure you, no man is stronger than an old-fashioned lumberjack.

The final step in my preseason physical training consists of multiple steps that are carried out throughout the year. And literally, this step in the process consists of lots of steps. For, each night, as I make my way around the house, every step is made on my tip-toes. Aside from allowing the wife to get a good night's sleep so she can continue her life as a teacher, these steps allow me to rise a step above as a hunter. No, I don't walk on the toes to get a better view. Rather, the technique allows me to slip through the forest (and the home) nearly silently.

By making each step at home on my toes, I'm constantly training, building my balance and the muscles in my legs so that, when necessary, I'm able to walk on my toes through the woods for unlimited distances.

This practice is probably the biggest key to finding success while deer hunting in the big woods. A quiet approach is usually the most important factor in being in the right place at the right time. Because the fact is, even if you're in the right place at the right time, if you made a big commotion getting there, you probably blew it before you even arrived.

As November advanced, my training was nearly complete. No longer was the daily 1.7-mile hike even a remote challenge. It was just a warmup. For the pure joy of immersing ourselves in the autumn woods, we found ourselves expanding our daily hikes to well over two miles. It was exhilarating to hike those hills with that dog, taking in all the sights and sounds and smells, feeling the rains and breezes, and absorbing the fresh fall air in the north woods. And to be able to go for miles, day after day, without the slightest feeling of fatigue, we were the healthiest horses in the county. Lean and mean at a solid 175 pounds, I felt as strong as ever for the challenge ahead.

22 THE IMPORTANCE OF THE RANGE

With less than a week until the 2016 season, all my ducks were lining up. The boat was stored, the wood was made, the leaves were blown, and the cupboards were stocked with food. It was down to the final countdown. A top remaining priority was that annual trip to the rifle range.

It was a brisk and windy day at the shooting range. With the place all to myself, I set up and began the sight-in process. At fifty yards, the first shot was good. On out to 100 yards and to my surprise, I missed the target entirely. So back to fifty I went, and now my shots were going several inches high. I shot more and found the same result. Reluctantly, I pulled the cap off the scope and made a slight adjustment. I wasn't really wanting to change anything, but the situation dictated otherwise.

After my initial adjustment, my shots went higher yet. Counting my clicks backward, then moving the crosshairs further yet, I tried another shot. Getting closer. After a few more shots and adjustments, I was on. At 100 yards, I managed to drill three consecutive shots to within an inch of the bull's-eye.

Now I carried some confidence. If I was going to get a shot this year, without a doubt, it was going to be right on target. I cased the gun and headed home, closer yet to my destiny.

Of course, the key to success in most jobs is to be fully prepared. Often, a key component of proper preparation is to make sure all the tools are ready for the day's work. In hunting, perhaps the most important tool is the weapon. And one of the most important responsibilities of the hunter is to make sure he's comfortable and efficient with his weapon.

Yet, in today's busy world, it's pretty easy to overlook this critical area of preparation. Because if we take care of our rifles, we find that most every year, they shoot fine right out of the case.

Usually, taking a few shots at the range is merely a confidence builder. Often, there's no actual sight adjustment involved. But sighting-in the gun is a step that should be—must be—taken each and every year. I learned this lesson the hard way back in 2014.

From the time I bought my rifle when I was 12 years old, the sights were never adjusted. The Remington Model 7600 and its iron sights were right on, right out of the box. For years, decades really, I shot that gun at the range before the season and nothing ever changed. It was always right on target out to 100 yards.

For the 2012 season, I decided to get smart and adjust the iron sights so the bead would lay in the bottom of the notch, instead of the original setup with the bead on the imaginary line across the top of the notch. As I was getting older, my near vision was starting to go and I thought this would be a more positive sighting setup. The adjustment worked well for the first couple of years. No more trying to find an imaginary line in the moment of truth. Taking the guesswork out of it, I felt like I was a much better shot with my brilliant "improvement."

Then complacency set in. Having successfully tagged mature bucks in nine of the previous eleven seasons, I was starting to think I had it all figured out. I'd learned where and how to hunt the big woods, and success was now a regular companion. I was thinking I was the best hunter I'd ever been. And that's partly true. Unfortunately, I started to overlook the details.

Knowing I'd always shot well, for the 2014 season, I never made time to sight-in my rifle. Even after I saw an old-timer talking on the TV about the importance of the annual sight-in, I talked myself out of it. Why bother, I thought. I'm pretty busy and nothing ever changes anyway.

Why bother, you ask? I'll tell you why. Just to be familiar with your weapon. That's why. So that, in the moment of truth, when your heart is pounding and you're not thinking quite right, you're able to operate in an efficient manner. You need to be so familiar with the routine that you can carry it out without conscious thought. Because in that moment of truth, you won't have time to think about all the little things that should come automatically. And that's just what happened to me.

A Lesson Learned

The day was November 21, 2014, in the year of the huge mid-November snowstorm. The previous day while hunting on public land west of Hardwood Lake, I found a big rub with bark shavings on top of the snow. It was obvious a good buck had been there within the last few hours.

Before daybreak the next morning, I was back in the area, sneaking toward the fresh sign found the day before. With a moderate snow still falling, I carefully snuck through the aspen saplings in the gaps between the balsams and oaks that interspersed the hemlock ridges of the area.

Shortly after daylight, as I crept through the thicket, I spotted a deer feeding less than fifty yards in front of me. Unaware of my sneaky presence, the antlerless deer was walking away from me, intermittently nipping at the buds along the path. I held up and watched as the deer eventually continued to the west and out of sight. After a few minutes, I resumed my stalk, quietly following in the footsteps of the deer who'd just departed. It wasn't fifteen minutes or fifty yards later when I spotted another deer, ahead of me and to the right.

Standing behind a snow-caked clump of saplings, I could see the outline and occasional movement of a larger deer, less than fifty yards ahead. I froze in place and watched intently as the deer slowly crossed from right to left in front of me. As he passed through a small opening, I could see it was a buck. My heart rate jumped a notch as I strained for a better look at his head. With another few steps forward I could see he was more than just a spike-horn. I readied my gun and held still, waiting for more info. After a few minutes, he proceeded forward and into a larger opening. Through the snowy trees I could see he had a decent rack, maybe a six or small eight-pointer. He lingered in the opening, then looked straight away. While I didn't have a scope on the gun, I could see well enough through the snow and saplings to notice he had at least three points on his left side. My heart beat faster as I realized this might be the moment. He took another step forward, and I got a clear look at his head.

Noticing his right antler broken off just above the base, it certainly wasn't the curly-tops I was looking for. And yet in this season of record-breaking snow, I had the feeling this might be my one and only chance of the year. With the heavy snow clogging all the woods in the area, this spot was one of the few places I could access for hunting. And with such limited options, I knew the opportunities at bucks would be few and far between this season. It was the first buck I'd seen, and in normal years I wouldn't even consider taking such a small buck. But the fact was, I wanted some venison and this was as good a chance as I could hope for.

I raised my gun and leveled the iron sights on his shoulder. It was an easy shot opportunity with the deer standing broadside at forty yards, completely oblivious to my presence. With a steady squeeze of the trigger, the sound of the blast filled the forest and the deer dropped like a ton of bricks.

I got him. While it was no trophy, I was happy to have gotten a buck on such a great hunt during such a difficult season.

Hoping to find and keep my lucky shell casing, I began looking for the brass in the snow. Searching in the thigh-deep powder snow, the mission was futile. I pulled my knife and began to blaze a sapling to mark the spot for a spring retrieval. As I carved the bark off of the nearest small tree, motion to my left caught my attention.

There in front of me, my deer was struggling to get up. I grabbed my gun and watched as the deer got to his feet. Taking careful aim at the now wobbly walking deer, I carefully fired another round. With the shot, the deer continued forward and started moving faster. Not too concerned at this point, I calmly took aim and followed the deer as he moved through the brush. As he entered another opening I let another shot fly. All that did was get him moving faster. Still following him with my sights, I found the next opening and touched off another round. With that, he started bounding. I ran a few steps forward then stopped as he ran through another opening. Taking careful aim, I squeezed the trigger to send my last shot. This time, the hammer came down on an empty chamber and the deer scurried on and out of sight.

What in the world just happened? I knew why my fifth shot fell on an empty chamber. Right away I recalled that I had racked open my chamber when I was looking for my lucky empty shell. When I did that, I ejected a live round and had failed to replace it. The real question was, how in the world did he get away after I dropped him on the first shot and then took three more close shots?

Figuring this was just a temporary setback, I reloaded my rifle as I made my way to where the deer had disappeared. He was gone. There were a few tracks, but no blood trail. Did he fall somewhere and I missed seeing it? With nothing to go on, I decided to go back to where he was when I shot.

Sure enough, I hit him, he went down, and there was some blood where he fell. But it really wasn't much blood. I followed his tracks and the spotty blood trail for about 100 yards. I was on full alert, fully expecting to see him up ahead at any second. After 100 yards, nothing. Another 100 yards, then a quarter of a mile, and still nothing. Oh, I was on his track all right and there was a little blood, but it wasn't looking good. The blood was sparse, a drip every twenty yards or so and there was no indication he was slowing down. I wanted to slow down to let him slow down, but with a steady snow falling, I risked losing his track if I didn't stay right on it.

I pressed on, and the marathon was under way. Within a half mile we'd crossed the next road to the north and sloshed across a creek. An hour later we were still at it when we crossed another creek and headed east toward the main road. Just short of that main road, the deer curled north, then back to the west and followed upstream along the high bank of the stream. It was on. The cat-and-mouse marathon.

A mile or so upstream, still on his blood trail, I looked ahead and saw a deer. Excited to finally find him, I raised my gun and prepared for the shot. Unable to see his head, I held my fire and waited for positive identification. It's a good thing I held off because when I finally saw that deer's head, it was a doe. Within moments, her fawns appeared and my tracking job hit a delay. I waited for the family unit to pass, only to have them approach to less than ten yards before spooking.

Now with a clear path to progress, I continued on the trail of my buck. Traveling upstream, I proceeded another half mile before I saw movement to the right.

Incoming. Moving down from the north through the hardwoods I watched a whole string of deer make their approach. Passing about sixty yards to my east, the deer, six in all, crossed my tracks and dropped into the cedar studded creek bottom. As the last of the group passed, I heard the distinct sound of a buck grunt and focused my attention back to the north. And there he comes, a paltry little buck. With antlers no more than two inches long, he was a pipsqueak. Yet he had all the gall and ball of a big bull, chasing those does for all he was worth, hoping to get a piece of the action. I watched him pass then resumed my own chase.

At midday, we were a couple of miles west of the main road and heading into the abyss of a dense cedar swamp. At this point, the blood was almost nonexistent, save for a drip every fifty yards or so. By now, it was clear that my shot was not going to make a quick kill.

By mid-afternoon I found where the buck had bedded. And by the looks of the blood, which was high in the cupped-out bed of snow, it was obvious my shot had hit high. My only guess was that the shot had found its mark high on the deer's back, above the spine. That would explain why the deer dropped with the shot as well as why the blood was sparse and high in the bed.

Dejected, I trudged on, hoping against hope that I might be able to finish the job. Late in the afternoon, I found myself continuing on the track south and west from Secret Lake, some four to five miles beyond the beginning of my day. Heading south now, the deer approached the creek again, passed by a couple of hunting camps, then turned to the west. Not long after that, we crossed a familiar road and the buck continued onto private property.

Wanting to respect the landowner, I left the track and continued down the road to my old friend's camp. I hadn't walked a quarter mile down the road, and along came Pug as he did his afternoon snowplow run. He stopped and we talked for a few minutes before he invited me to warm up in his cabin.

He hadn't gotten a buck yet this year, but was happy just to be at camp after suffering a heart attack earlier in the year. I explained my situation as I warmed up in the cozy creek-side cottage. While sharing my story, along came Pug's buddy Rich. I went through the story again and was refreshed by the response of my fellow hunters. Of course I was welcome to track my buck on Pug's land and, as a bonus, his friend Rich volunteered to assist in the search.

For the late afternoon, I set off again to track the buck. Following until dark, I never caught up with the deer and left the track for the night. Being the good Yooper sportsman that Pug is, at the end of the day, he was kind enough to offer me a lift, saving me from a four-mile hike back to my truck.

By the next morning I had snowshoes and returned to the track. Having traveled nearly five miles inland from Lake Superior, the snow level showed a steep increase. While the snow down near the lake was about knee deep, the snow up there in the hills was easily up to the belt line. There would be no traveling through these woods without snowshoes. It was a noisy and clumsy affair, making my way on the big feet through the tight corridors of the mountainside thickets.

By mid-morning I'd found the buck's night bed and the tracks he made in hastily vacating the area when I approached. With just a bit of blood in the bed and none flowing upon his exit, it was abundantly clear that the deer would survive my initial shot. I tracked through the day, progressing another couple of miles west and farther up into the hills. By the end of the day, it was obvious there was no way I would ever catch this deer. He knew I was on him and he'd returned to nearly full strength. The only way I might catch him was if I were a wild and hungry wolf.

Frustrated and exhausted, I returned to Pug's camp where I'd parked that morning. I dropped in to share the results of my findings. After sharing the evidence, Pug agreed it had to be a hit that grazed the deer's back, with the shock so near to his spine causing the initial drop. Pug was as gracious as could be, even taking the time to share a similar story he'd lived through. But I still felt stupid. After I beat myself up pretty good, Pug concluded that stuff like that has happened to every hunter.

The one point that George curiously raised was the key question. He put it to me something like this: "You might want to ask yourself, why'd ya miss?" It was a good question and before long the answer came to me.

Thinking back, I recalled the adjustment I had made on my sights two years prior. That was it! I hadn't thought about it since I went to the range last year. And this year, in my complacency, I'd skipped the range. The next day I tested the theory and, as suspected, I found that when I aimed using the old sighting set-up, at forty yards my shot landed about eight inches high. With the new sight set-up, the shot was right on. Now it was obvious. In the moment of truth I'd failed to think about my new sight set-up and instead, my actions were automatically flawed as I took aim just as I had for the past two decades.

Having skipped the sight-in step this season, I'd forsaken the opportunity to find my flaws. In doing so, I'd missed the key reminder about my previous changes and thus failed to be fully prepared. I knew better and I was ashamed.

This time it was I who played the fool. More than my embarrassment, I felt terrible for wounding an animal as the result of my own complacency. Never would I let that happen again.

I spent the remainder of my season in futility, trying to find and finish that small half-racked buck. Not that I really wanted to spend my time that way,

A field test revealed the reason for my 2014 miss. Using the old set-up, my shots went high.

but the way I roll, if I draw blood, I look at that as my deer. In my mind, I can't justify going and embarking upon another hunt until the current hunt is complete. As is the policy in many guided big game hunts, my personal policy is, I won't attempt to harvest a second animal until I've done all that can be done to harvest the first one. Needless to say, it turned into a long and frustrating season, searching diligently for that half-racked cripple.

As it turns out, I finally did see that deer again, on the penultimate day of the muzzleloader season. Driving back toward the area where I'd left his track some days previous, late in the morning I spotted him. Less than seventy yards from the road, he hung around just long enough so I could get a good look at him. Unusually spooky, after less than a minute, the deer tucked his tail, dropped his head, and quickly snuck off and out of sight. Out of a sense of duty, I took up his track and followed him the rest of the day. I never did catch up with him again and that was a good sign. It was obvious he was alive and well, fully ready to face the challenges of the winter ahead. I wished him well as I turned and called off the chase. Though it apparently wasn't too severe, I was sorry I'd hurt him and hoped he'd make a full recovery.

After thirty years of hunting with a rifle, it was only the third buck I had wounded and lost. And yet, it was now three too many. For weeks, the memory of the whole ordeal stuck in the back of my mind like a nagging toothache. I was completely to blame and I was disappointed in myself.

The reason I share this little story is, I hope others will learn from my mistakes. Stuff happens, even to the most experienced hunters. Sometimes it might be a scope that gets bumped. Other times, it might be a change in ammo that changes everything. Once in awhile, as in my case, we might even outsmart ourselves then forget about it.

For a whole lot of reasons, it's imperative for every hunter to practice with their weapon every year before taking to the field. Out of respect, we owe it to ourselves and the animals we pursue. Bottom line? You need to practice. Every season. Especially when you think you don't need to.

23 PRESEASON SCOUTING

The final steps in my preparation for the 2016 season were taken on Saturday, November 12. Looking back, these proved to be some of the most critically important steps in my journey. In retrospect, had I not taken these steps, it's clear everything would likely have ended differently.

Preseason scouting has traditionally not been near the top of my priority list. Each year, Dad asked before the season if I'd been out in the woods doing any scouting. And each year, my response was always the same. In my mind, it really didn't matter where the deer were before the season. What mattered was where they are during the season. Besides, I usually try to employ the element of surprise and thus strive to leave my hunting spots undisturbed before the season. With that philosophy, I had always saved my time and energy to do my scouting while hunting.

But for some reason, that same question from Dad kept ringing in my ears. Perhaps it *was* a good idea to scout before season. It sure seemed like it this year. Wanting only to hunt for the Legend, I decided to actually do some preseason scouting this year, hoping to find some sign of his return.

So that Saturday I decided to take a good hike through the Legend's known territory from last year. Accompanying me on this scouting mission would be Special Agent Cajun, my best friend, the pound hound. Making our way to the Legend's mountain, we found little deer sign, zero buck sign, and a complete lack of acorns. Without the acorns, it was a different place. Where the whole mountain was littered with tracks, droppings, scrapes, and rubs last year, this season the area had almost no deer sign.

Over the hill we ranged, then down the back and around to the east. Making our way along the old logging road through the hemlocks, I still had yet to find any buck sign. Then I found it. Along the trail, under the low-hanging branches of a large hemlock, I spied the remnants of a recently worked scrape.

Under the hemlock, this was one of many scrapes tended annually by the Legend.

It was an impressive sight. Nearly three feet wide, it was a reworking of one of the many scrapes maintained the previous year by the Legend. Oftentimes, scrapes will show up year after year in key locations, regardless of which particular bucks are in the area. While I couldn't be sure if it was the Legend who'd worked it this year, it sure was encouraging to see.

Proceeding east, we continued on the route formerly maintained by the Legend. Taking a trail to the south, we made our way through an old clear cut, then looped back to the west on the south side of the mountain. As we approached another hemlock with low-hanging branches, I was hoping to see the accompanying scrape with renewed activity. And sure enough, when we got there the ground had recently been worked over. Now this was a big scrape, clearly made by a mature buck. Along with the deeply carved scrape, there were several major rubs within sight. It was a good sign. A very good sign indeed.

Perhaps he *was* back after all. Walking along the old logging trail, there were numerous patches of sand and bare dirt, all of which held a good number of fresh deer tracks. Then I saw exactly what I was looking for. It was a tremendous deer track. While it was obvious the deer was merely walking, the hooves pressed deep into the dirt and at a width of nearly four fingers. It was the sign of no ordinary deer. Among the many average-sized tracks, this one stuck out as a giant. No doubt, the spoor was left by an animal of at least 220 pounds.

A little farther up the trail, I found a huge rub, one that could only have been made by a dominant buck. Continuing west along the Legend's secret path, I found another, then another, then one more fresh scrape. Less than a quarter mile from where I'd missed the Legend last year, his sign for the new year looked familiar. Without an actual sighting or video evidence, I couldn't be completely sure of it. Yet in my mind I kept hearing this little voice repeating over and over. He's baaack.

After locating that final cluster of scrapes, we quietly made our way back to the truck. It was just what I wanted to see. As we made our way home, my hopes for the fast approaching season were quietly being launched into the upper stratosphere. Perhaps there would be more to the story after all.

With all the preseason priorities achieved and all the preparations complete, I was ready to go. In the last days leading up to the season, I placed my traditional good-luck phone calls to my dad and brothers. While they were all sticking with their annual plans to hunt their tried and true traditional spots, I had other plans. In my conversations, I reported that it looked like the Legend might be back and that my mission was to double down in the sole pursuit of that one particular deer.

My plan was to pull the plug on my old spot and focus on the Legend. It was a risky proposition. I'd hunted my usual Opening Day spot at Secret Lake for each of the past fifteen years and had taken some of my best bucks on those days. It was a spot I knew well and a spot I knew was good. The decision to switch spots was made easier by the fact that I hadn't seen a single deer at Secret Lake in the past three years. Saw some wolves, but no deer. That, combined with the fact that I'd never in twenty years seen a true monster buck there, made it almost easy to change the plan.

So the new plan was on. I would focus all my efforts on the Legend. During my scouting walk with Cajun, we'd built a little brush-pile blind alongside the Legend's scrape line. While it was an unproven spot, my plan was to be there well before daylight for the Opening Day sit. I didn't quite know what to expect, didn't expect much really, but I was excited to at least be hunting in the Legend's territory. Unsure if he really was back, I was happy to at least have the opportunity to perhaps find out. If he was still out there, I was going to do all I could to find him.

I told my brothers just that. I wasn't sure if I'd ever get another chance at the Legend, but I was determined to work harder than any hunter ever had before. If it could be done, I was going to be the one to do it. I was ready to go, ready to do what must be done, and willing to put in all the hard work it would take.

24 GAME ON

November 15, 2016

For this Tuesday Opening Day, the forecast called for cloudy skies, light winds, and temperatures hovering around thirty-eight degrees. Later in the day, meteorologists were calling for some light rain, then clearing overnight. With the weather having yet to transition to a winter pattern, it was shaping up to be a pleasant time to be in the woods. No major snowstorms in the forecast, no heat-waves, just good moderate hunting weather. While the lack of snow would curtail any sort of tracking activities, that same lack of snow would allow for easy foot travel to the deepest corners of the woods and would reveal any buck sign made within the last month. Certainly, the conditions could have been much worse.

After the typical one-eye-open night of sleep on Hunter's Eve, I was up and at 'em before 4 a.m. Even with less than two hours of sleep in my system, I was alert and excited for the day. After eating a good breakfast and taking a shower, I made a solid lunch for the road and prepared my gear. By 5:30, I was in the truck, headed out for the half-hour drive to the land of the Legend.

Arriving at my parking spot just before 6 a.m., I began the slow march through the deep woods to the Legend's mountain. Less than 100 yards into my hike, I spooked a deer and stopped to listen as it bounded off into the dark forest. I didn't think much of it as it's not unusual to spook some deer on the way in, no matter where you go. After a half-hour hike I finally arrived to my preselected post for the Opening Day.

With the weather a trifle warm and having overdressed, by the time I reached my hide at 6:30, I was sweating like a hog on a hot summer night. Hunkering in the dark under the big hemlock tree, I quickly disrobed, tossing aside my soaked undershirt as I stripped to the bare belly. Glazed in sweat, my white torso seemed to glow under the ambient light of the cloud-dispersed super-moon. The cool morning air felt good on my overheated body, and within minutes my core temperature had been regulated. By 6:45 I was back in full uniform, ready for the day to dawn.

The first light of the day was greeted by my eager anticipation. For the deer hunter, opening morning is the time when hopes are at their highest. Having waited a long year for this day to come, each moment is filled with the hope, the belief, that any minute now, that big buck might show up.

Thinking back on previous years, the seasoned hunter will recall all of the success found on Opening Day. This in mind, it's no secret that the hunter's best chance for scoring will likely show up before late morning. By the end of the day, the odds of finding success for the year will begin a steady statistical decline. With that, the first day is always exciting, even when there's nothing to see.

And nothing to see was exactly what was coming my way. After the first shooting light arrived a little after 7, it was more than an hour before I saw any signs of mammal life. A little after 8, a red squirrel came along and paid a visit, hopping up on the log two-feet in front of me for a closer look. After he went on his way, I waited another hour without seeing anything. Yet another hour came and went, and I was starting to fidget.

By 10, after having seen zero deer, I couldn't take it anymore. Still being a little damp from the morning hike in, a chill had settled into my bones.

After hours of waiting and nothing to see, I moved on from this Opening Day hideout.

Not helping matters was my still ailing backside, which made sitting in any one spot for more than an hour an excruciating exercise. More than that, I was just plain bored. Seeing nothing moving and knowing the Legend was out there, somewhere, I could hardly stand the thought of waiting any longer. I had to get moving.

While the conditions for sneaking weren't perfect, it wasn't bad either. Methodically, I placed each footstep, careful to proceed as quietly as possible. Heading east, I made my way down the ridge and into the canyon separating the Legend's mountain from fifteen-point Mountain.

Recalling a favorite scraping spot for the deer of past seasons, I made a side trip to the trail that hosted some low-hanging hemlocks and the annual accompanying scrapes. Sure enough, as expected, the usual scraping spot was active again. Less than a half mile from the Legend's mountain, this was the area where I first found that huge track during the 2013 season. Could this be one of the Legend's signposts? I had a feeling it might be.

By this time, the day was moving into the afternoon. Knowing I was in a good area, I decided to find a place to quietly spend the remainder of the day. A hundred yards south of the scrape, I took a position under a big spruce, on the top of a wooded knob that rose up perhaps 100 feet above the surrounding forest. With a view out to almost 100 yards and nearly 360 degrees of coverage, it was a splendid spot. Not only were the visuals great, but the habitat was prime.

It was an area between two creeks, in a hollow between three mountains, with several old logging grades converging amongst the dense growth of pine, oak, balsam, and hemlock. With the nearest road access miles away, not surprisingly, there was no sign of any other people having been here. Better yet, the area was decorated with a healthy supply of fresh scrapes on the ground and big rubs on the nearby saplings. Sitting on that knob, I could hear the thunder of the waterfalls and rapids surrounding me. I waited it out till dark, fully expecting to see deer show up at any time.

Unfortunately for me, the day ended the same as the previous three Opening Days had, with exactly zero deer sighted. I suppose it'd be easy to get discouraged having gone four straight years without seeing a single deer on Opening Day. However, having hunted for decades in the U.P., I've learned that when you do it the old-fashioned way, without bait or a blind, that's the way it goes sometimes. I wasn't all that discouraged, but I was starting to get the feeling it was going to be another long year.

At dark I began the long uphill climb of several miles back to the truck. It was a slow process, but after more than an hour I made it to the home stretch for the truck. Not really trying to be stealthy, I was startled when I jumped several deer less than 100 yards from my rig. I stopped and listened as they bounded off into the brush. I couldn't tell how many, but there were several deer in the group, maybe four or five. As they ran off, it sounded like there was a real heavyweight in the group. As the big beast shook the ground with his bounds, my ears picked up what sounded like antlers bumping against trees. And there it was, again and again as the deer retreated into the distance.

It was a sound unlike anything I'd ever heard, save for those times when I watched a big bull moose beating a hasty retreat. While I knew it was no moose in there, I couldn't help wondering what exactly I had heard. Could it have been the Legend? In my mind, I pictured his wide antlers careening off the brush as he bounded through.

Arriving home, I shared the story of my Opening Day with a keenly interested wife. "Doggone it," I said. "I had all dang year to think about, plan, and prepare for the season. All year, and all I can come up with is a big fat nothing on the Opening Day."

Nothing, that is, except for those few deer I spooked right by my parking spot. I couldn't understand it. Wondering aloud, I questioned why in the world would those silly deer be hanging around by the road. They had no reason to be there, unless, of course, they had a reason.

Then the wife piped up. "They had every reason to be there," she mused. "Every season, around this time, all you hunters head out to the woods, park your truck, then walk way back in the woods to do your hunting. Actually, those deer have you hunters figured out. They know the safest place during the hunting season is by the hunters' parked trucks."

Dawn laughed at my ignorance. It was funny to hear her make such an astute observation, and she did have a good point.

I thought about it for the rest of the evening. Why were those deer there? There had to be a reason. Maybe it was as simple as the wife suggested. Or maybe there was another reason. Had some hunter moved in and thrown down a bait pile? Or was there a hot doe in the area, attracting a crowd of potential suitors.

Whatever the reason, I grew more curious as the hours passed. Perhaps it was the strange sound I heard as the deer ran off that had my mind racing. It sure sounded like lots of sticks clunking around as those deer bounded away. Not sticks, really. It actually sounded like antlers bouncing off the trees.

Now I've never really heard a deer sound like that before, but that's just what it sounded like. The noise echoed in my ears and my imagination filled my minds eye. I could see the Legend, back and bigger than ever, pin-balling his way through the thicket. Closing my eyes with my mind filled with images of the Legend, sleep would come quickly on this night.

25 THE BIG DAY

November 16,

The beep-beep-beep of the alarm startled me awake at 4 a.m. I lay there a
few moments, adjusting to the arrival of consciousness. Without much
delay, I was moving, preparing to emerge into the cold. At 4:04, my feet hit
the floor and my day had just begun. After taking Cajun out to the tree, I
made my way to the breakfast table. As I crunched my Total cereal, my
thoughts went right to the daily question. Where to go? With dozens of
favorite spots spaced out among a thousand square miles of hunting
territory, where to go is always the toughest question. Guess right, and the
day is golden. Guess wrong, and the precious day is wasted.

Within two hours, I was ready to walk out the door. Making my way up to
the truck, I was carrying all the gear I might need for the day, including my
waders. After seeing the fresh scrape yesterday down by Fifteen-Point
Mountain, I was thinking about making my way across the creek and into
that section. On the fringe of the Legend's territory, it's one of my best
spots and I was eager to get in there.

I made one more trip down to the house to give the wife a big hug before
heading out. Waiting for me at the door, she greeted me kindly and gave me
a warm embrace as she wished me good luck. Happy to have her support, I
headed out into the day carrying an aura of positive energy.

Riding into the darkness, I began to think hard about my plan for the day.
With a forecast for light northwesterly winds and temperatures in the high
thirties, I thought twice about my idea to cross the creek and head for
Fifteen-Point Mountain. That might be a good plan, but it would be better
with a south wind.

The more I thought about it, the more I was drawn to that sound I heard
last night as I made my way back to the truck. A northwest wind would be
perfect for sneaking into that area, as the trail heads in to the north and
west. With the woods soft and drippy from the rains overnight, it would be

a perfect morning to quietly sneak in to just about anywhere. And that noise. That strange noise I heard as those deer ran off last night. I just couldn't stop thinking about it.

Even if my interpretation of the racket was simply the product of an overactive imagination, the fact remained: There were deer in there during both of the past two nights. And whatever it was, it was certainly more than a doe and a couple of fawns in there last night. Why they were there, I couldn't be sure. Whether it was someone's bait pile or a hot doe that had brought the deer together, whatever the reason, they were definitely there.

Half the battle in hunting deer in the big woods is finding where the deer are on any given day. One day they may be here, the next day there. Finding where they roam and accurately predicting where they may move on any particular day is probably the most difficult aspect of the hunt. But if you can get into the middle of the mix, you're already halfway to success.

As I drove through the darkness, my thinking evolved and I began to lean toward returning to the area of the first day's hunt. My thought was, if they were there yesterday morning and they were there last night, then maybe, just maybe, they would be there again today. And so the plan evolved. I just had to figure out why those silly deer were hanging out by the road.

Hoping the deer would still be in the area, the plan was to sneak back about three quarters of a mile to a key crossing, wait there till midday, then make my way back up toward the road for some further investigation. I wasn't sure exactly where I would sit for the morning, but I was shooting for a sneaky spot near a small marsh where the aspen and maple thicket transitioned to the oak-studded mountainside.

While I had never hunted in this particular spot, it was an area I marked on my mental map last year as I explored and charted out the territory of the Legend. Situated just off the logging road where an older grade intersected, it was a key crossing, confirmed by the presence of three major scrapes in the clearing and a plethora of rubs on the surrounding saplings. In my mind, it seemed like the perfect spot, a natural crossing corridor, just the perfect distance from the road, and adjacent to some of the best habitat for miles.

I killed the lights and quietly eased to a stop in my familiar parking spot along the side of the road. Emerging from the truck into the dank air of the damp morning, I gently eased the door shut until the latch clicked. With a nearly full moon poised to drop to the western horizon, the woods were aglow with a faint light, casting a web of shadows on the forest floor.

From the very first step, I was on my tip-toes, creeping with the silence of the wind as I moved away from my transport. I hoped those deer were still nearby and knew if they were, regardless of how quiet I tried to be, I knew they would still hear me. My only hope for success was to sound like a deer as I passed. Chit-chit-chit, I tiptoed my way along the trail, trying to precisely match the sound and cadence of a traveling deer. Moving in bursts of about seventy yards at a time, I was careful to not go too slow, not too fast, and cautious to not break too many sticks. Even in full darkness and without the use of a flashlight, with the ambient light of the moon I was able to place each step carefully enough so as not to cause a commotion.

By 6:30 I had stealthily covered the three quarters of a mile and arrived at the little clearing. Looking for a concealed place to sit, against the faint glow of the night sky, I spotted a big spruce at the edge of the clearing and headed that way. Arriving at the spruce, I quietly cleared the damp leaves from the base of the tree, making a bare dirt pad just large enough to sit quietly upon.

The only problem with this spot is the few spruce branches hanging down at the base of the tree. Dry and dead branches, these twigs would certainly interfere with my comfort, mobility, and potential for clear shooting. I thought, I can fix that easy enough. I grasped the first offending twig at its base on the tree, about shoulder high, and broke it off.

SNAP! Ouch, that was loud. I paused a moment, then grasped another of the problem branches. CRACK! Oops, that's no good, I thought. That'll never do. Way too noisy on this silent morning. Every critter within a mile is gonna hear that. I better quit while I'm ahead. Then I thought about my racket a little more. Maybe, to another deer, I might've sounded like another buck making some kind of trouble. Maybe, if I quit now, all might not be lost.

Abandoning my plan to sit under the spruce, I got back on my toes and began to sneak a few yards to the west, looking for a better spot to sit. Moving about ten yards, I found that spot, a little hump at the base of a large maple on the edge of the clearing. After brushing away the leaves for a quiet place to sit on the ground, I pulled my seat cushion from my pocket and made myself comfortable. In the darkness, it was difficult to tell exactly what the visuals would be like, but it was clear I would have a good view of any deer crossing the clearing directly in front me.

At 6:45, I was settled in, ready for whatever the day had in store. With my water and lunch beside me and my rifle in my hands and on my lap, I began to tune in to the forest around me. The rain of the previous night had given way to clear skies, leaving the forest dank and dripping.

Seated on the cool and damp forest floor, I could hear drips dropping for nearly 100 yards in all directions. Closing my eyes, my ears took over and with each drip, the long forgotten muscles of the ears strained to turn toward the fleeting sounds. Feeling like a dog shifting his flaps to focus on the sound of distant howls, I could sense my ears moving like a radar dish to pick up the blips.

At the foot of the large maple, this is the spot where I chose to sit on 11-16-16.

I opened my eyes and looked to the setting moon and its surrounding stars, then looked back to the east at the first hints of dawn. I reached out with my right hand and touched the trunk of the maple under which I sat. It was a strange sensation. Perhaps it was just my imagination, but I swear I could feel some sort of energy amongst the trees. It was almost as if the energy of my touch on the tree had spread up the trunk and out the branches, connecting to the neighboring branches and emanating out in all directions. I pictured lightning spreading from tree to tree, branch to branch, and spreading out through the forest through all of the connections of intertwined life.

To the south, the sound of a lone owl announcing the conclusion of the night carried through the still morning air. With 6:55 came the sound of a duck, quacking out his communication from the ponds situated about a quarter mile to the west. Now that was interesting. It's not too often that I hear the sound of ducks during the deer season. Usually they've all headed south by mid-November, but apparently with the warmth of this season, there were still some stragglers. It felt nice to share the forest with some feathered friends.

With the forest around me just coming to life and into the light at around 7, I heard what sounded like a piece of birch bark rustling somewhere in the distance, maybe a half mile to the southwest. A few minutes later I heard the faint sound of movement in the forest, again, maybe a half mile to the southwest. Listening intently, I focused the radar in that direction.

At about 7:10 I heard the unmistakable but faint sound of an animal moving, somewhere down to the southwest. Chit-chit-chit, it sounded like a deer walking. Listening intently, I heard it again. Chit-chit-chit. Incoming!

With the sound growing as the animal approached, I tightened my grip on my rifle. Straining to see in the half light, I peered into the shadowed forest. Chit-chit-chit. It's definitely coming this way. Moving at a steady pace, it sounded like a deer all right. As I focused on the steadily approaching sound, it was beginning to sound like a familiar one, like a single deer moving right toward me at a brisk walk.

Now, anyone who's hunted for long enough has heard that sound. It's as unmistakable as the day is light. It's the sound of a buck who's on a mission. Unlike does, fawns, and normal deer, the rutting buck walks through the forest at a steady clip and without pause. Where the does and young'uns will walk slowly, regularly pausing for a bite to eat and to check the safety of the situation, those big bucks march steadily along. Careless of anything other than does during the frantic weeks of the rut, those big bucks seem to have a destination in mind and waste no time in getting there. This march of the bucks is most frequently carried out during the first minutes of daylight, when the marauding bucks sneak away from the nighttime rutting grounds to the safety of their chosen bedding areas.

It was a sound I'd heard just last year on the second day of the season. Unfortunately for me, as it sometimes happens, the deer last year made it past me a few minutes before shooting light. Had he crossed five minutes later, I would've been in business. As it was, that deer was just barely successful in making it past me and to his safe spot. And I was left to wonder what he might have looked like.

By 7:15, the moment of truth is upon me. Chit-chit-chit-chit, the sound of the deer approaching steadily draws nearer. I look to the southwest and strain to see the source of the sound. At fifty yards, I see movement through the maples. Chit-chit-chit-chit. At forty yards, I see the outline of a large animal walking. Chit-chit-chit. At thirty-five yards, I see the shape of a large deer, quartering toward me and coming quick. Chit-chit-chit-chit. Now thirty yards away, it crosses through an opening, and I see it's a really big deer. At twenty-five yards, it crosses another opening and I see what looks like the biggest buck I've ever seen. I blink my eyes and see it again. It's an impossibly big buck. Inconceivably big. Chit-chit-chit.

By now the deer has crossed in front of me, left to right, and is passing to my right, out in front of me. Being a right-handed shooter, this put me in a tough situation. Not wanting to shift my position with the deer at such close range, I keep my butt planted on the ground and twist to my right, then raise my gun.

At this angle, it's impossible to get the butt of the gun seated firmly against my shoulder, so I ease the butt of the gun past my shoulder and lean to the right to look through the scope.

Chit-chit-chit. I look into the scope, find the buck and focus on his head. Again, I see what looks like the biggest buck I've ever seen. Impossibly large. Without a second thought, I move the crosshairs down his neck and find his shoulder.

Chit-chit, BOOOOOOMMM!!!

In the orange flash of the muzzle blast, amid the half light of the dawn, I see the deer crumble before me. As the ringing in my ears clears, I can see the fallen beast a little more than twenty yards in front of me, his white muzzle pointing to the sky. Without so much as the slightest twitch, the deer lay there motionless as the light of day evolves.

After a few moments, I detect what feels like sweat on my brow. I dab at the moisture and feel a distinct stickiness. My senses rapidly returning now, I also notice the growing welt on my forehead where the scope had bitten me. Here we go again. I knew I took a good one this time, but none of that matters now. What matters is what lay before me.

I sit there in silence, trying to conceive of what had just taken place. Could it be? The Legend? I don't believe it. It couldn't really be what I thought I saw. Because what I thought I saw was an impossibly big buck. Maybe it really was the Legend of Thunder Canyon.

Dropped in his tracks, it was certainly a huge deer down. Could it be the Legend?

At 7:20, all I could see was the shape of a big animal down and his white muzzle pointing to the sky. At 7:30, I raised the gun and looked to see what it was. Still too dark for confirmation. At 7:45, I looked again, and again, all I could see was a big deer down. Even with the scope cranked up, I couldn't see any antlers sticking up. Maybe my eyes were playing tricks on me. Maybe it was just a nice little six-pointer or whatever. It couldn't be as big as what I thought I saw. Could it?

Then I started to second-guess myself. It couldn't be a doe. I was sure I saw horns, and yet, now I saw nothing. Was it a mirage? Was it my imagination that had put huge horns on a little buck or could it really be a buck as big as I thought? It couldn't have been a doe, and yet I still wasn't seeing anything for antlers. I looked again. I wasn't quite sure where the horns went, but I was sure I had never seen a larger deer on the ground.

By 8, it was fully light and I took yet another look. Sure enough, it was a humongous deer. And there was his big white muzzle, pointing to the sky. But where were the horns? Scanning the scene, I could see the deer had fallen over backwards with his back to me and his head had fallen straight back into the leaves and brush where he stood.

Now in the full light, I scanned the scene and saw what might be antlers. Carrying the correct shape and color, it almost looked like the tips of the main beams sticking up. Except these supposed points were way too far apart to be normal deer horns. Looking closely, it was starting to look good.

As daylight filled the valley, I could see what looked like an abnormally big set of antlers.

At the base of the maple, the shell casing where it landed and the notebook I wrote in.

I think it was then that the reality of the situation hit me. The first wave of emotion hit as I realized it might actually be the Legend. I knew what I saw and, though it was unbelievable, I was starting to believe it.

Surprisingly, it wasn't a feeling of intense joy. There was no touchdown dance, no victory celebration at all really. Rather, it was more a subdued sense of satisfaction with a little bit of sadness as reality slowly took hold. I pulled my journal from my pocket and began writing.

11-16-16 - Wednesday. 48°, NW winds, clear, super-moon setting.
6:00, Leave house.
6:20, Arrive at Legend Trail.
6:45, Sitting east of beaver pond.
I think all night & mornin' about the deer at the parking spot. Maybe there's a hot doe & buck in there. Then I think: fool's gold. It's stupid to hunt that close to the road, but ... but! That's where the deer are.
So I decide to sneak in the trail past where they were, then wait for them to head for the hills in the a.m. I tiptoe all the way in and decide to set up in the clearing where the scrapes were, just east of the pond. In at 6:45, I wait under the super-moon for light to break.
Just before light, at 7:00, I hear an owl, then ducks on the pond. It's a good omen. A few minutes later, I start to hear sounds in the

distance. I close my eyes & let my ears take over, shifting and focusing on the sounds & drips of the morning. In a couple minutes I hear a sound to the SW. I wait & listen & then I hear it. It's a deer. Incoming!

Seated at the base of a large maple, I get my gun ready. Sure enough, he's coming from my left. I can hear him clearly & he's approaching at a steady pace. Chit-chit-chit. It sounds like a buck.

At 50 yards I see a dark shape cross through the timber. At 40 yards I can see the dark outline of a big deer. At 30 yards, I see what looks to be a huge buck.

It's still pretty dark, but with the clear sky and the dawn rising behind me, and with the super-moon setting, it's just light enough to see. It's him. I raise my gun & look through the scope. In a split second, I see his huge rack & move the crosshairs to his shoulder. Safety off, I squeeze the trigger.

Booomm!

In the orange flash of the muzzle, I see him crumple, a mere 20 yards before me. Dead as a stone, he never moves an inch. The weight of the massive rack caused him to tip over backwards. Falling nose to the sky, the last thing he saw was the stars above.

Rest in peace old friend. I'm sorry it's over.

And so it was. The Legend of Thunder Canyon finally fell. I'm sad for him. While I'm humbled and thankful to have had this opportunity, today I shed tears of joy and tears of sadness.

By 8:15, a full hour after I shot, I could take the suspense no longer and decided to walk over to my fallen quarry. With only twenty-two steps to the downed deer, at the halfway point I could see that it was in fact a huge buck. As I came around the front of the expired animal, my suspicion was confirmed. No question, it was indeed the Legend of Thunder Canyon.

After shooting some video of the scene, I sat quietly with The Legend. I thought about my journey, about his journey, and about our convergence here in this time and place. For years, each of our steps had led to this one final moment. My heart and soul was filled with feeling.

While there was some excitement in having achieved my goal, there was as much a feeling of sadness. Sadness in seeing such a beautiful creature lying dead before me. Sadness in knowing that our adventure was over. Sadness in knowing the Legend would no longer walk these trails. And a bit of remorse in knowing that, in claiming my moment of ultimate victory, my old friend had to lose his life.

He was a respected and revered opponent whom I thought of every day. After all this time, as happy as I was to have claimed victory, I was equally sad to have ended his life.

Seeing such a beautiful animal dead on the ground can bring on strong and mixed feelings.

It was a bittersweet moment, a moment that would likely leave me changed. After having killed the deer of my dreams, I wondered if I'd ever have the appetite to kill again. Claiming victory by taking his life left me feeling uncomfortable. If I could have healed him in that moment and sent him on his way, I would have done so.

The whole thing seemed surreal. It was the first deer I'd seen all season. To think of all the places I could have chosen in my 1,000-square-mile hunting territory. To think of all the places he could have been in his nine-square-mile range. To think that our paths would converge in this exact time and place. It was almost inconceivable. To think of all the trails he could have chosen, all the turns I could have taken, and yet, here we were.

After I regained my composure, I fished out my phone and attempted to call the wife at work. I was surprised to get a couple bars of signal so deep in the bush. As she answered the phone, I tried to share the news.

It was difficult to talk. Emotions swirling in my soul, I was bathed in some indescribable state of shock where each word came with a struggle. Choked up with joy in having finally achieved the ultimate goal in hunting and anchored by the sadness in my heart of having taken such a legendary life, I was nearly torn apart by the conflicting emotions. It took all the manly strength I could muster to tell the basics of the story.

The Legend of Thunder Canyon, in the clearing where he fell.

"I got him," I told her. "I got The Legend of Thunder Canyon."

"No way," she said.

"Way."

"Are you sure it's him?" she asked.

"No doubt."

"How big is he?"

"He's huge. A giant. He's just an eight-pointer this year, but he's the biggest damn eight-pointer I ever saw. His rack is about two feet wide and he's got to weigh at least 200 pounds. He's an absolute monster." Still filled with emotion, I fought to retain my composure through the call.

"Congratulations, Buddy," Dawn said. "I'm so happy for you."

"Thanks, Buddy. I couldn't have done it without you. Thank you." I forced the words from my throat as tears welled up in my eyes.

After calling the wife, I thought about who to call next. Knowing my dad and brothers would be in the field hunting, I considered calling Mom to share the news. As much as I wanted to tell her, I couldn't burden her with having to keep the secret until I talked to Dad.

The only person I could think to call at the moment was my brother-in-law Mark, who, unfortunately for him, was already back to work so early in the season. As I munched a part of my sandwich, I dialed the phone. Well into the workday, Mark was quick to take the call. I told the short version of the tale as I continued chewing my lunch.

The excitement over the phone was palpable. With Mark's enthusiastic hoot cackle as he laughed out loud, the thrill of the moment was amplified. It was all I could do to tell the story without choking. After completely turning Mark's day upside down, I went back to the Legend for a few quiet moments.

It almost seemed too easy. Except it wasn't. Sure, it was only the second day of the season and it was already over. By previous standards, the season was a cake walk, over nearly as soon as it began. The fact that I had barely suffered this season seemed to make it all too simple. But simple it was not.

The fact was, this was no ordinary deer and it was certainly no ordinary hunt. For that matter, I was no ordinary hunter either. Because for the past year, I thought about the Legend each and every day. And it was not just a few passing thoughts. It was a full-on focus nearly bordering on the obsessive. Many a day I had spent working on Part I of the book, writing, editing, talking about it, then working on it some more. And every day I'd made conscious efforts to prepare for the next encounter with the Legend.

I thought about all the miles I'd walked to supplement my strength, all the steps taken on tip-toes to build my balance, all the hours I'd spent in reliving and telling my story. And that was just in the last year. Never before had I worked so hard in the course of a hunt.

The author with the Legend at the conclusion of the hunt.

Digging deeper, I reflected on all that went into my efforts of the previous season and all the seasons before that. It had been decades of hard work, all in the hope of someday standing in this moment.

I always believed that someday I'd get a huge buck in the big woods and yet, when the day arrived, the reality seemed surreal. Even through the disappointment of my failure from last year, I always believed the Legend's path and mine would cross again. I just never imagined it would end like this.

The Work Begins

After a while, I set forth with the task of field dressing the deer. Taking on a clinical approach, I began the ages-old task of preparing the meat for consumption. In one way, it was an unpleasant task, but at the same time, it was a small part in the bigger picture of survival. I wondered how the cavemen felt when the time came to butcher the mammoth.

Survival and sacrifice is a story as old as time itself. It's how life has gone on for eons. Big fish eats little fish, cat eats mouse, wolf eats deer, man eats chicken. Having grown up on a small farm, I came to see the connection of life and death at an early age and from close up. I tried to be thankful. For now at least, sustenance would be continued.

It occurred to me that there would be much less meat consumption on earth if each consumer were forced to kill and clean the meat they eat. It's not easy, and it's really not fun to kill and butcher. What is it then? It's real.

Killing forces a person to appreciate life, both living and dead. And if we do it with full comprehension, it inspires us to kill less and let live more.

After field dressing the deer, I wiped off my hands and prepared to place the kill tag on the animal. While it's never particularly fun to remove the guts from an animal you killed, I was proud to be one of the few remaining humans in touch with the old world realities of eating. In today's world of fast food and thoughtless meat consumption, I was happy to be fully connected with the reality of life, death, and survival in the natural world.

As I bent to punch the appropriate information on the tag, I felt the presence of something, or someone, nearby. I raised my head to look around and there, fifty yards away, stood another hunter. It was the first hunter I had seen in the woods in four years. It looked to be a younger fella though it was no one I had ever seen before. Without really thinking about it, I spoke out loud.

"Ian?" I asked.

The orange-clad hunter smiled and nodded his head. I waved a big wave, inviting him over to share the moment. While I'd never met the guy, I knew right away it was the fella who'd left the note on my truck last year. As he arrived at the scene, I extended my hand and introduced myself.

"Hey, Ian, I'm Duane Pape. Great to finally meet you in person."

"I'm Ian," he said as we shook on it. "Good to meet you."

"What are you doing here?" I asked.

"I was hunting a couple miles away and I just started thinking about this spot," he said. "I hadn't been here all year and I just had this strange feeling I should get over here and check the place out. ... So, at 9 o'clock I picked up and headed over here. I saw your truck parked there and I figured I might as well head back and see what was going on. And here you are."

We both marveled at the strange coincidence, that he would just happen to walk right to me after not having been to that spot all year. The timing of it seemed pretty remarkable.

We walked over to the buck and Ian knew right away.

"That's him. That's the Old Mountain Buck."

"The Legend of Thunder Canyon," I corrected him.

"Congratulations on getting the Legend," Ian said. "If anybody was gonna get him, I'm happy you did. You earned it."

I was honored by his kind words and impressed by his elite level of sportsmanship. After he took a good long look and touched the magnificent buck, we walked over to where I sat for the hunt and I took him through the whole story.

Seated in the very spot where I had taken the shot, I went through every detail of the morning. It was a good time, sharing a hunting story in the moment and on the scene with a complete stranger.

In no time, it was clear that Ian was a good guy. As he told the details of his experiences with the Legend, I could see that he was a guy a lot like me. Rather than being territorial, or spiteful, Ian was happy to simply have had a role in this amazing hunting story.

Having shared our stories and set the solid foundation for a lasting friendship, my new friend was kind enough to take a few pictures with my camera. With the completion of the photo session, Ian even volunteered to help drag the brute out of the woods. As I rigged the critter for the long haul, Ian got a call on his phone.

A broad smile filled his face. In the still woods, I couldn't help but overhear the conversation. The excited caller on the other end told the story of how he himself had also taken a nice buck on this same morning.

After the call, Ian happily informed me that the caller was his dad. It seems his dad had been hunting close to camp and, shortly after Ian had headed over this way, he'd dropped a good buck down by the creek.

Ian reiterated his offer to help with hauling out the Legend. I thanked him for the offer, but politely declined. I had all day to get the job done.

"Besides," I told him, "you need to go and share the special moment with your dad and help him out."

Taking a call in the woods, Ian gets the word that his dad also got a buck on this morning.

Before departing, Ian was kind enough to help drag the Legend to a cool and shady spot. I thanked him for his help, and more than that, for his good nature and good sportsmanship.

It's guys like him that make hunting a great experience in the big woods of the Upper Peninsula. Unlike some of the locals who play stingy defense on the public lands surrounding their private property, Ian was a fellow hunter happy to share the time and place. For guys like us who share a common bond and common ground, it's more about camaraderie than competition. I was thankful to have forged a friendship with such a quality young man.

As he started to leave, I thanked him again. Before he left, I told him someday it'll be his turn to get a legend of a buck. I only wished that when the day came, I could be there to help and be a witness to his hunt of a lifetime.

After he walked away I shook my head in amazement. It was almost too much to believe, the way the day had evolved. It was a miracle of fate topped with an ironic twist based upon an unbelievable saga of a story. My mind tried to grasp all the variables that had just come together. How on earth could everything have worked out so perfectly?

Indeed there was an energy in the woods that morning. Was it just good luck? Was it a miracle? Magic? Coincidence or convergence? Or was it the work of a God or the Great Spirit?

Maybe it was some help from my recently departed deer-hunting grandma. Or maybe it was my spirit guide, Moose, the ghost of my beloved hunting partner and long since departed yellow lab.

Whatever it was, it seemed plausible that perhaps there was some sort of unexplainable energy guiding our every step on that fateful morning. While I like to think I did everything right, the fact that it all came together so perfectly seemed almost unbelievably unreal.

After Ian headed out to help his dad, I got on the phone looking for some help of my own. Sure, I had all day to get the job done, but I knew it would be a long haul to get that huge deer out of the woods. A little snow would have helped immensely. As it was, I found myself nearly a mile from the road, with nothing but bare ground over which to tug the massive buck.

My first call for assistance went to my old friend and hunting partner Brad. Being busy running his own business, he's not hunted for several years. Yet, whenever I've called him in past years, he's always been willing to help out. That includes a difficult midnight drag that I summoned him for during the 2013 season. On that mission, we dragged a 170-pound eight-point more than two miles, over mountains and across rivers, all in the dead of night amidst a powerful wind storm. After all that, it's a wonder he even takes my calls anymore. But that's what good friends do.

Being the good businessman he is, he was prompt to answer my call on the third ring. In the middle of completing some paperwork and estimates, he was gracious in taking the time to hear my story. While he did have an estimate to complete on this particular morning, he offered to help later in the afternoon. Looking at his schedule, he figured that he could be there by about 4 p.m.

"Perfect," I told him. As a matter of pride, I wanted to do as much of the work as possible myself. Yet I knew there was no way I could load the buck in the truck on my own. I explained where he could find me and told him to take his time in getting there. I had plenty of work to keep me busy for the day. I thanked him for taking my call and for making the time to help.

Then the real work began. Don't get me wrong. Compared to all the effort that went into actually getting the Legend, the task of hauling him home was a relatively minor undertaking. Yet the fact remained, the job ahead would be a big one. With my first attempt, I tried to face forward, hoping to drag the deer behind me. I coiled my muscles then lunged forward. At the end of my rope, my progress was halted before it began. I could barely budge the beast. Again, I tried and again got nowhere. Oh boy.

Not willing to give up, I adjusted my approach and tried again. This time, I faced the deer and pulled backward, almost like the anchor man would do in a traditional tug-o-war. Heave, ho. I broke the dead weight from its anchor of gravity and tugged with all my might, taking short choppy power-steps as I backed my way up the trail. Counting each grueling step, I pushed myself to the limit and paused after completing thirty-three strained steps. Breathless, I paused and bent down to rest from the strain. This was going to be a long haul. After a few minutes of recovery, I had at it again, tugging and toiling for all I was worth. Again I pushed to the limit and went a few more steps to complete my thirty-three step burst. This might take a while.

Already glazed in sweat, I paused to shed a layer. Not wanting to carry any more weight than necessary, I walked about 100 yards up the trail and dropped my heavy coat and extra gear. With my load lightened and my core cooling, the next burst was a little easier. With the deer flat on his back and the rope lifting his enormous rack off the ground, I was able to haul him for another thirty-three small steps backward. With a few more bursts and rests over the next hour, I was able to reach the spot where I'd left my extra coat and gear. Again I advanced my surplus gear another 100 yards then returned to the deer for the next segment of the journey.

Arriving at the deer, I was taking a drink from my water when my attention was caught by movement in the woods to the south. I watched as a deer crossed through the hardwoods about 100 yards away. As it quickly walked through a few openings, it looked like a buck. I waited and watched as it disappeared into a thicket to the west. After a few minutes, the deer emerged into the clearing where I had slayed the Legend just a few hours previous. I raised the gun and looked through the scope. Sure enough, it was a buck.

Though he was now almost 200 yards away, I could clearly see horns. It looked like small eight-point, but the thing that stuck out was the fact that all of the points on the top of his rack appeared to be broken off. I guess that's what happens when you trespass on the Legend's turf.

I never considered shooting, despite the fact it would've been perfectly legal to harvest that deer too. Rather, I hoped that in a few years, perhaps that deer would be the next Legend of Thunder Canyon.

It was a fine sight to see. While I've heard many stories about guys seeing another buck while they're dragging one out, it was my first time in thirty-three years that I'd seen another buck while dragging one out. If nothing else, the beautiful sight confirmed what I already knew: I had stumbled into a pretty good spot.

Back to the drag, I continued with my grueling process of tugging thirty-three backward steps, then stopping and panting for a few minutes, then repeating. With my perpetually bad back, along with the strain came the pain. It was nothing new. The pain from my mid-April back blowout had never really gone away. It was just something I had to deal with. So heave ho, here we go, grit and grin and bear it. On and on, I pulled, pulled, pulled.

Along the way, as it turns out, in the strain of the day I blew out the sole of one of my favorite old boots. The cost of doing business, I guess. And why not? A blown-out boot goes perfectly with a blown-out back. In either case, the prospects of a prompt repair are dismal. So we soldier on, holding to the mantra that if it doesn't kill us, hopefully it'll make us stronger. If nothing else, if I survived this daunting task, I was sure to end the day a stronger man.

By 3 p.m. I was starting to see the light at the end of the tunnel. Drawing ever closer to the road, I could now hear the occasional truck as it rumbled past. Slowly and steadily, I worked my way to within shouting distance of my destination. With a few more cycles of pull and pause and pant, I finally drew to within sight of the truck.

Now running low on H2O, I took a break from the work and walked the remaining quarter mile back to the truck for more water. After I loaded my extra gear into the truck, I sat for a snack and swig of water in the shade of the rig. I hadn't been seated for five minutes when a vehicle approached. On the wings of perfect timing, it was my buddy Brad, ready to lend a hand. After greetings and gear gathering, we made our way to the fallen beast.

As we arrived at the deer, Brad's face gave way to a big grin.

"It's the big guy. He's huge. Wooow," Brad exclaimed.

After a recap of the story and a brief photo session, we set to the real work. And fortunately for me, the work had just gotten much easier.

Nearing the end of the drag, The Legend seemed to get bigger with every step taken.

Being the well-prepared and thinking man that Brad is, the guy was sharp enough to bring along an appliance dolly for the final haul. While the hand truck was a little short for the extra long deer, the tool worked like a charm. After carefully placing the animal on the cart, when we lifted his massive head we were able to get the deer fully off the ground and took him the rest of the way out on wheels. It was a fraction of the difficulty of dragging on the ground, but still no easy task. After about fifty yards we took a break, then resumed the haul.

Within minutes we were at the truck with our bounty. And while simply rolling that deer was tough, getting him loaded into the truck would be even tougher. Now it's one thing for two men to try to lift a 200-pound deer into the back of a truck. It's probably triple the challenge to work that same animal into the back of a compact pickup truck with a cap. It just barely fit, but without much room to maneuver the animal. We managed however, and by 4:30 I was out of the woods and in the truck, with the Legend along for the ride.

Now you might think this is where the story ends. But if you've ever harvested a buck of a lifetime, you know the story is just beginning. Unlike many of the hunting videos we watch on YouTube, the reality is, there is so much more to a deer hunt than just the kill shot.

Seeing The Legend from this angle takes me back to the days I watched him get away.

My old friend Brad admires the Legend after we loaded him into the truck.

Of course there's all that goes into it leading up to the shot, but there's often just as much work to be done after the animal is on the ground. After you get the buck out of the woods, there's the hanging, the skinning, the butchering, the taxidermist, and, of course, there's an incredible story to be told over and over again.

The Ride Home

The first place I headed after I thanked Brad was back into town. My top priority was to get hold of my old friend Joe, the guy who originally shared photos of the Legend with me. Arriving in town, I was able to give him a call and was surprised when he answered. I told him I was hoping to stop by his camp, that I had something for him. Already hosting company, Joe asked if I could drop by another time.

"Actually," I told him, "my situation is sort of time sensitive. I'll cut to the chase. Remember that big buck that I missed last year?"

"Did you get him?"

"I did. It's such a special deer and you had such a key role in my story, I thought you'd want to see the Legend in person."

"Yeah, okay. You can come on up, but if you could wait until after dark, that would be great. I've got some hunters out there now and I don't want to mess them up."

"That's fine. I'll go into a holding pattern then stop in just after dark."

"All right. We'll see you then."

Before the day even began, I was already hoping to see Old Joe. He'd had a pivotal role in the creation of Part I of my book, and I'd been carrying around a draft of the book with Joe's name on it for days. Having mentioned him by name and having used some of the photos Joe had so kindly shared, I felt it was important that he receive a copy before I had the thing published. Besides, I was proud of my work, thankful for his contribution, and eager to share the masterpiece with my friend.

Arriving at Joe's camp shortly after nightfall, I was greeted by the host and a few of his old-time hunting buddies. After the introductory handshakes, I presented the manuscript to Joe and thanked him for his contribution. Next on the itinerary was the retelling of the story of my day. Still in shock from the whole experience, I was beaming with enthusiasm as I described the details of the morning. Acting out every key moment in the story, my animations came to a crescendo as I sat on the floor and reenacted the moment of truth when the buck made his final approach.

My audience was patient and polite as I shared the riveting story. I was sure they had enjoyed hearing the story as much as I enjoyed telling it. Yet the moment they were all waiting for was the walk out to the truck for a look. Without further ado, we stepped outside to see the buck. As we gathered around the truck, right away Joe knew it was the Legend.

"Yep. That's him," Joe declared confidently. "No doubt, that's him. Did you get a measurement of the spread?"

"Not yet. I'm guessing at least twenty-two inches. Maybe more."

"Well let's get a tape measure. I've got one right here in the garage."

We went back to the truck and looked at the tale of the tape. At twenty-three inches, there was still more to go. While it was tough to get the exact measurement by the light of flashlight, it was clear the buck carried nearly two feet of inside spread.

"Have you guys ever seen a bigger one?" I asked.

"We've got some big bucks over the years, but never anything quite that wide. He's a good one all right."

"Did you guys see him this year or get any photos?"

"Not that I know of. We didn't get the cameras out till late in the season, but as far as I know, he hasn't been by here this season."

"Congratulations," Joe said. "You earned him. If anyone was gonna get him, I'm glad you did. That's one heck of a buck."

"Thanks, Joe. I did earn him. But it's nice to hear it from you. More than that, thanks again for sharing the photos. If you hadn't shared the pictures, the story wouldn't have been the same. Now, I feel sorta bad for taking him. Hopefully you guys will have some luck this year and hopefully, next time, it'll be your turn to get that big buck."

As I headed on my way, I wished the guys well and thanked them again for being such good neighbors and sportsmen. "It's guys like you," I told them, "that makes the U.P. such a special place."

My next stop on the way home was at Big John's camp. Since it was right on the way, I had to stop in to share the tale. Rolling up the long forest driveway, I was happy to see lights on in the old artifact-adorned camp. Walking up to the cabin, I was greeted by an open door and a friendly hello.

I passed under skulls, antlers, and assorted logging artifacts as I entered through the doorway. The heat of the woodstove was a fine welcome to a hunter coming in from the cold.

Sitting in the guest chair, I heard the report from John and his brothers Gerry and Ted as they ate and relaxed at the small camp table. Somewhat surprisingly, they hadn't had any luck yet, but it was still early in the season. Following their brief and uneventful report, John looked at me and laughed.

"Looks like you did some shooting this year. Did that scope get ya again?"

"It did," I said. "Big time. You ready to hear my story?"

"Let's hear it."

"So you remember last year, how I told you I missed that huge buck?"

"Yep. And didn't that scope bite you in the forehead last year too?"

"Yah. Anyways. As it turns out, I ended up writing a book about that whole debacle. ..."

I went into the long version of the tale, starting with the recap from last year, then progressing all through the events leading up to and including this fateful day. As I reached the part where the Legend approached, I sat on the floor and faced to the northwest, just as I had done during the morning hunt.

"Chit-chit-chit, here he comes," I said as I reenacted the scene. With the story still being so hot off the press, the excitement in the storytelling was palpable. Fully engaged in the moment, every face in the camp was alight with smiles as I shared the suspenseful and exciting details of my hunt.

"What a great story," John commented.

"Congratulations," Gerry piped up. "Have you got him in the truck?"

"I do."

"Well let's go have a look," John said, as we rose to our feet.

Outside, we rounded the back of the truck and I opened the back window of the capper. Dropping the tailgate, the Legend was revealed.

"Wow," the guys exclaimed. "That's a monster. How wide is he?"

"Inside, it's more than twenty-three inches. Outside, better than twenty-five. Have you guys ever seen a bigger one?"

"Not that wide. That's a heck of a buck. Congratulations. It's just nice that a real hunter got him and that he didn't get shot over a bait pile. You earned that buck. You should be real happy."

131

"Oh, I am, all right. And I thank you guys for your part in this whole thing. I remember distinctly, last year in my moment of defeat, you guys lifted me up. You told me I'd get him someday. Well, your confidence in me helped me to rebuild the confidence in myself."

I thanked the guys for being such good hunters and sportsmen. "It's guys like you," I told them, "with similar ethics and values, that makes hunting in the U.P. such a great experience." We chatted a little more before I wished the guys well and headed for home.

After all this time in a long and exciting day, I had yet to make it home to share the story with the wife. Rolling down the long hills, I slowly made my way along the dirt roads, savoring the moment as much as I could. It was a ride I'd always hoped to make, like a victory lap and the parade after the win. Riding along the trail through forested hills in the final stretch to home, the reality of it all began to hit me. Thinking about everything I'd endured in this epic hunt, the failures and frustrations, and now to be heading home victorious, I was overwhelmed. The road ahead became distorted as the tears burned in my eyes. I couldn't wait to tell my sweet wife all about it.

Clunking my way up the stairs and into the house, I found the wife waiting in her chair. She stood to hug me, and as she laid eyes on me she gasped. The wound to my forehead was now swollen to the size of half an apple and was topped with a nasty crescent shaped gash, the blood from which now dried and caked into what appeared to be a crusty festering wound.

"What happened to you?"

"I just had the greatest hunt of my life. That's what happened to me."

"Are you okay? Do you feel all right? Do you have a headache?"

"Honestly," I told her, "I couldn't feel any better."

I fell into her arms and we squeezed each other.

"I got him, Buddy. I got him," I told her.

In the comfort of her loving arms, I could no longer keep the powerful emotions bottled up. As I began to tell the story, I choked on my words. I paused to regain my composure, then picked up where I left off. Again, as I went into the story, my voice cracked and I had to pause. Tears welled in my eyes and I choked up. There was no use in fighting it. The emotions were strong and real, as powerful as can be. Trying to be the tough guy, I was never going to get through the story.

As she held me, I continued on. No holding back the flood. I delved forward into my narration, laughing, crying, choking and hiccuping all the glorious way. By the time I was done, my emotion had spilled over into her spirit and her eyes filled with tears. She held me as the tears streamed down my face, and I trembled with the power of the feeling.

THE LEGEND OF THUNDER CANYON

Now I knew how all of those Olympic gold medalists had felt when they went home to share their victory with their loved ones. To have worked so incredibly hard for something and to achieve the impossible goal, after struggle and sacrifice along the way, then to bring home the gold and share the glory with those you love the most, it was one of the most stirring moments of the entire four-year odyssey. I was happy all by myself out in the woods, but to share the thrill with my best friend, that thrill of victory was amplified exponentially.

"Congratulations, Buddy. I'm so happy for you," she said as she hugged me tight in an extended embrace.

"Well, where is he?" she asked. "Let's go have a look."

I took her by the hand and we went downstairs and out the front door. I turned on the lights and led her to the back of the truck. Opening the tailgate, she was greeted by the stunning sight.

"Holy shit!"

We both laughed as the surprising words fell from the beautiful lips of the otherwise proper princess. It was an apt response, and she wouldn't be the only one to utter such a reply.

She touched the regal stag and marveled at both his size and beauty. Never had we seen anything like it. It was a moment of awe, not unlike the time I brought home the bald eagle I found in 2010. The sight left us speechless, seeing something we knew we would likely never see again. We lingered in the moment and hugged again.

"I'm so happy for you."

"Thanks, Buddy. I never could've done it without you. Thanks for helping to make my dreams come true."

The next item on the agenda was to spread the news to my family and friends. The first phone call went out to Mom and Dad, my biggest fans and best supporters. Mom answered the phone and we talked a little about the weather and more about how the guys did there in lower Michigan.

Next on the line was Dad. Turns out, he also had a great start to the season as he was able to tag a nice eight-pointer on the first morning. I offered my congratulations and told him how happy I was for him. How nice, at 72 years old, he was able to enjoy another Opening Day of deer season, this time sharing it with my brothers and their children.

Then came the big question.

"How's your season going?" Dad asked.

"Well, I've got a story to tell, but we're gonna have to get Mom on the phone so I can tell you both at the same time."

As the conference call commenced, I started with the details of the first day, then moved into the second day. Taking the time to share it all, I carefully recounted every pertinent detail of the adventure. From the deer I bumped in the dark on the first day, to my thought processes overnight, to my approach the next morning, then on to the moment when I heard the big buck approaching, I explained it all in glorious detail.

"Chit-chit-chit-chit." I described the scene as it all developed before me. As I neared the moment of truth, I could again feel the emotion building. When I got to the part when I shot and the deer fell, tears filled my eyes and I struggled to continue.

"It was him," I told them. "It was The Legend of Thunder Canyon. I got him. I got the Legend. ..."

My breath taken away, I choked on whatever words I still had to say. Fighting to hold it together, I had to pause, for I could no longer speak.

"Wow," Dad said. "Congratulations. I'm so happy for you."

Only later did I learn that my emotion was contagious, for as I struggled through the tears to tell my tale, so too did my loving parents have their own tears of joy. It was a special moment to share, the 400 miles of distance between us bridged by the shared emotion found in the thrill of victory. In that moment, we were as close as if we were in the same room together.

After that thrilling call, I made one more call on the night. This time I called my neighbor Jeff, with the hope I might get some help with hanging the huge deer. Without telling him why, I asked if he could come over. I suppose I may have given away the surprise when I told him he might want to bring his camera. Being the good friend Jeff is, he was here in a jiffy and ready to help. Before he could see the Legend, I corralled him to the front yard fire pit where I had him sit in the chair for a little story-tellin' session.

I went into the story, recalling the hunt from the first day before going into the main event. Just as I had previously, I was sure to include every significant detail, trying to deliver my friend to the scene of the moment. Leaning forward on the edge of his seat, Jeff smiled continually as he hinged on my every word.

"... And I saw what looked like an impossibly big buck, the biggest I ever saw. ... I moved the crosshairs to his shoulder, and boom. ... After an hour I walked over and I could see it was him. It was the Legend of Thunder Canyon. I got him, I cackled. ... I got him!"

"You got him. Wow. I can't believe you got him. Congratulations."

"I can't believe it either. You wanna see him?"

"Heck yeah. Let's go take a look," Jeff said.

"Wow," Jeff said as I opened the back of the truck. "He's huge. The Grand Poohbah. The Big Kahuna."

We had a mini celebration then set to the task of hanging the beef. It was a good thing Jeff was willing to help. Even with a double pulley system, it was nearly impossible to get the deer up and off the ground. Only with a little extra oomph were we able to get him up in the air.

We stepped back and admired the gigantic animal. It was the biggest deer I'd seen in thirty years and likely the largest Jeff had ever seen. After a few more minutes of savoring the moment, I thanked Jeff as he headed home.

Now in the last hours of the evening, my day was finally done. Exhausted by sleep deprivation, the extreme effort of hauling the beast out of the woods, and the pull of the powerful emotions, I was ready for some rest.

Sleep came easy that night as it was one of those times when you don't even remember the head hitting the pillow. Instantly out, my unconscious mind swirled with dreams of the details of the day just done. In my sleep, I relived it all, retracing each key moment in a dream so real, at the moment it was indiscernible from reality.

Talk about living your dreams. After the nightmares that haunted me following last season's debacle, waking to remember this night of sleep would be like watching a dream come true.

26 AFTER THE FACT

November 17,

Finally, it was over. No more up at 4 a.m. No more walking out in the woods an hour before daylight. No more waiting around all day for nothing. For the first time in three years, it was a perfectly good day for deer hunting and I would be staying home for the day. Even though I had a combo license making it perfectly legal for me to take another deer, I was all done. The drive that pushed me so strongly forward for all these years was now completely gone. For all I cared, I might be done forever. Certainly, at this point, I couldn't even conceive of killing another deer. Not this year anyway, and maybe not ever.

Instead of hunting on this day, I slept well into the day, then took the time to hang around with the pound hound. We ate a feast fit for kings, laid around on his mom's bed, then took a healthy hike through the hills.

Making my way through the hills, I wore my earpods as my iPod blasted out my favorite songs. Attached to the harness of the pound hound, I howled my way through the hills like a blue tick on the trail of a tiger. Singing all the way, you'd have thought there was a concert in my neck of the woods. Certainly there was in my spirit, a signing of the spirit that echoed a joyful melody throughout the hills.

Perhaps that's why the wolf howls over his kill. Perhaps it's that feeling of satisfaction in having secured sustenance that's been fueling the songs of the forest since the first wolf-moon shone its light on the forest floor. I felt that satisfaction and let loose with my own nuanced howls, filling the hollows with a melodious mew.

In my case, anyway, it was an unbridled joy that led me to walking through the hills singing at the top of my lungs. Indeed I was having the time of my life, parading through the hills with my dog, and me, the human, howling all the way.

136

Continuing the stroll down the hill, the next song came on and I continued along like a one-man marching band. Crossing the road and making our way down through the yard, my bellow continued.

Rounding the corner of the house, I was surprised to find my beautiful wife, smiling in the fresh air of the afternoon. Continuing in song, my eyes filled with tears as I carried on for the newfound audience.

We hugged and danced, then walked to the water's edge. What a nice way to spend a mid-November day. It was the first time in years that I'd seen the daylight in my yard in the middle of the month of the hunt. Likewise, it was the first time in years I had seen my wife in the light of a mid-November day. I was happy to be home, to say the least.

Later, as we shared dinner, I told Dawn about my conversation with the reporter from the local television station who inquired about my story. Over the phone, the reporter on the other end of the line was eager to bring out a news crew to capture the story for the evening news. Declining the cub reporter's request for an interview, I asked instead to speak with Brian Whitens, producer of the local outdoors show "Discovering."

Knowing my story was worthy of more than a forty-five second bit on the nightly news, I wanted to share the tale with the guy who spends his life telling stories about adventures in the outdoors.

For the first time in years, I shared some mid-November daylight with my pack.

Graciously, the young reporter shared the contact info for Brian, then reiterated her desire to get right on the story. Again, I politely declined her offer to send the camera crew and thanked her for her interest.

After talking to the reporter, I placed a call to Brian Whitens. Taking my call during the mid-morning, Brian was at deer camp with his son and some friends. Without wasting any time, I broke into my story and shared the tale. As the guys at his camp leaned in to overhear the details of the conversation, I made my way through a brief telling of the experience. Later on, Brian told me that within a minute or so, he knew he'd be making the eighty-mile trip to see the Legend.

When I finished with my story, right away we started looking at our schedules. With plans to cover an annual buck-pole event scheduled for Friday night in Escanaba, Brian offered to visit on Saturday.

While that might work, I was concerned about the deer hanging for too long with temperatures in the mid-forties. My primary concern was getting the cape off as quickly as possible so it could fully cool. The plan was to skin the deer tomorrow and get the cape to the taxidermist the next day. Of course, it really would be best if we could do the interview with the deer fully intact. "Could we do it tomorrow?" I asked.

To my surprise, Brian agreed to make the long trip on Friday, despite the fact he'd need to be back in Escanaba later that night to film the stories at the buck-pole. So the plan was set. I could tell Brian was as excited to capture my story as I was to share it.

Next on the daily docket was to find a taxidermist. I had hoped to have my old friend John Carlson do the work. Unfortunately, I learned in a phone call that he just couldn't do the deer mounts anymore. After he did a superb job on the northern pike I caught ten years ago, I was disappointed he couldn't take care of the Legend.

Without another candidate in mind, I started calling around. A few calls in, I talked to Mike Anderson, a guy who runs a taxidermy business down in Ishpeming. When he told me he'd been doing this stuff full-time for eighteen years and he wasn't just practicing, I knew he had the experience to do the job right. I called a few more guys in the business, and soon, it was clear Mike would get the gig.

Later in the evening, I was able to reach both of my brothers by phone. Each time I told the tale, I took them to the scene of the action as I described every detail of the hunt.

Fully immersed in the moments of my memory, I practically came unglued as I arrived at the crescendo of the composition. In both instances, my throat knotted up and my eyes burned with tears when I got to the point in the story where I declared: "I got him."

As I told the tale to my brothers, the whole experience seemed like an out-of-body experience. Finally, I was the lucky one. Finally, everything worked out perfectly. And as I relived those critical moments of the hunt, the whole thing seemed surreal.

27 COMPLETING THE PROCESS

November 18: The Interview and the Weigh-in

By 4 p.m. Brian Whitens was here and we had just enough light to do a quick shoot and interview. While we got some good material, we knew there was much more to cover and a second interview would be needed. In the course of our meeting, I mentioned I had shot some video in the field and offered it up. Of course, Brian was interested. Knowing I'd need a couple of days to process the deer and the video and seeing as he had a show to produce in the next two days, we agreed to get together for another interview within the next few days.

After the TV interview, the next batch of work was upon me. I suppose, in a way, I live the old fashioned life. Unlike so many of today's hunters, who lack the time or will to process their own deer, I take great pride in cutting-up and packaging my own venison. It is a time-honored tradition, handed down to me from my father, and down to him from his.

Before starting with the skinning process, I hoisted the buck up on the scales for an official weigh-in. My guess in the field was that the deer would weigh at least 200 pounds. Honing in, I was thinking he'd tip the scales somewhere around 210 to 215 pounds.

Pulling on the pulley rope, it took all I was worth just to get his front end up to the maximum lift height. Even then, in my enclosed porch with an eight foot ceiling, his hind legs still carried a good deal of the weight. Getting creative, I was able to attach a rope to his hind legs, then lift the loop of that rope up and onto the hook of the scale. With just his tail brushing the ground, the scale told the truth of the tonnage.

I gave it a good bounce, and the scale settled back to its previously confirmed stopping point: 199 pounds on the nose. While I'd like to tell everyone he was 200 and some-odd pounds, the fact is the fact. He went 199 and not a pound more or less.

Before the skinning process, the Legend tipped the scales at 199 pounds.

What's also a fact is when I field dress a deer, I take great care to make sure the entire chest cavity and pelvic arch are completely cleaned out. Were I not so thorough, I'm sure the deer would have dressed out well over 200 pounds. As it was, according to the chart that accompanies my big-game scale, the estimated live weight of a 200-pound field-dressed deer would be 240 to 250 pounds on the hoof. No question, no matter how you measured it, the deer was huge, the biggest I'd seen in thirty years.

With the weigh-in complete, the next task was the skinning process. I'm not quite sure how I was able to do it by myself, but after a herculean effort, I was able to hoist the deer up to a proper skinning position. Using a gambrel device affixed through the deer's hind legs, I was able to get the deer to where his nose was just off the ground.

Having been just above freezing in the days since I harvested the deer, the hide was still soft and pliable. Starting around the hind legs, I carefully trimmed the hide, and began to pull it down. The skin pulled relatively easily, almost like shucking the husk off a corn cob. Aside from some temporary hang-ups near the tail and around the shoulders, the skinning went well. Taking my time to be careful not to cut through the hide, I was still able to get the job done within a few hours. Had it not gotten difficult near the top of the neck, the job would've been done in less than two hours. With the conclusion of the skinning, another busy day came to an end.

November 19 and 20: The Butcher Shop

There are many reasons I make the time to do the butchering myself, first and foremost being quality control. Now I'd bet that many commercial deer processors do a fine job. But I'm certain each morsel of meat that I package for preparation is of the absolute highest degree of quality. It's perfectly clean, free of any fur, fat, or connective tissue. There's no question as to whether it was kept at the proper temperature, whether it sat around too long, whether the equipment was clean, or whether the venison is actually from my deer. When I'm done, the meat I store and prepare is the finest wild-raised organic meat found anywhere. No hormones, no antibiotics, no artificial colors or flavors, simply 100 percent pure forest beef.

The other thing I cherish about processing my deer is the connection the practice allows me to have with the reality of life and sustenance. To see the whole process through, from the kill to the table is to fully understand the implications of the actions we take. No longer is meat a thing that's ordered through a microphone and delivered in a neatly packaged presentation from a toothy attendant behind some drive-thru window. My meat is real. And when I consume it, I understand where it comes from, the animal who sacrificed his life for mine, and the efforts that must be made in order to serve the proverbial burgers.

The butchering solidifies the connection between us and them, and exemplifies the core of the relationship between predator and prey. If done properly, in killing, one recognizes the value of the life of an animal taken. As the hunter lives to see another day, a certain sadness takes hold in knowing the adversary lives no more. It's in this delicate moment of natural balance when one is dealt a regulating mechanism to limit the desire to take any more than is needed. If you love life, you love to see living animals. And if you love to see the animals alive, you can't help but hate to see them die. And if you're engaged in the entire process, you learn it's so dang much work, you don't want to take any more than is absolutely necessary. It's only when it gets too easy that the gluttony begins.

Taking great time and care, I spent the better part of two days processing and preparing packages of pure venison for storage in my freezer and the freezers of a few select friends.

November 21: The Taxidermist

I suppose the ultimate tribute we pay to the animals we hunt is to make use of as much of the fallen animal as possible. When we cook and consume our prey, our lives are sustained through their loss, and in essence, they live on as a part of us. What remains after that are the spirits of our prey, our memories of the hunt, and the artifacts of our conquest.

To the greatest of those animals we harvest, we bestow the honor of everlasting reverence when we adorn our palaces with the mounted heads of those very beasts we slay. While rather morbid at its core, this curious practice is largely meant to honor a magnificent specimen. Thus, a trip to the taxidermist is often an exciting event included in the experience of a remarkable harvest.

For me, this would be my second time taking a deer to the taxidermist in thirty-two years of hunting. Ironically, my trip to the mount shop on this day came exactly thirty years to the day after I harvested that big buck when I was a kid. I've always thought about Mr. B.G. on November 21, and again this year, it was a special day, both in memory and moment.

My chosen taxidermist this time was a fella named Mike Anderson, owner of Green Creek Taxidermy in Ishpeming. When I arrived at his well-kept shop, I had a feeling I'd chosen the right guy. Upon meeting Mike, I knew I found the right man for the job. A big fella and just a couple of years older, with his friendly and playful personality he reminded me of my big brothers and wasted little time before he started to razz me.

It was a fun trip to the taxidermist. Despite having just lost their beloved dog, Mike and his wife were cordial and friendly, working together and willingly taking all the time I needed. The evening got even better when another fella and his wife stopped by to visit their friends at the taxidermy shop. Small world that it is, the guests who dropped in just happened to be a former coworker, Kevin, and his lovely wife. And lucky for them, they arrived just as I was beginning to recite the long version of my hunt story.

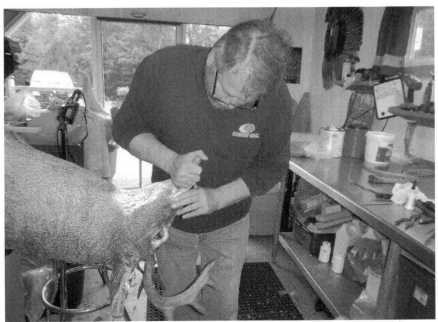

Taxidermist Mike Anderson works on another deer mount in his Ishpeming studio.

Gathered in the shop, surrounded by friends and furs, I once again relived the glorious moments of my hunt with an animated retelling of the tale.

After the storytelling session, Mike made his way to the work station and began the task of removing the hide from the skull. With the skill of a seasoned surgeon, he delicately trimmed away the skin from the bone, and within minutes the task was complete.

In addition to having a shoulder mount done, I elected to have the feet preserved and went ahead and had the back half of the hide tanned too. Being such a special deer, I just couldn't stand the thought of having any part of it go to waste. As I left Mike's shop, I looked forward to the day I'd bring the Legend home to stay.

November 22: Another TV Interview

Still processing the fruits of my harvest, this day was shaped around another visit and interview with Brian Whitens of the "Discovering" TV show. Having only limited time when we did the first shoot with the Legend, we agreed to get together again to discuss the story in its entirety. Having already processed the deer, this session would be filmed on location in the woods where I hunt.

Making our way up a nearby mountain, I shared a few hunting tips and demonstrated my tip-toe stalking style while Brian did a little filming.

Filming on location with Brian Whitens, producer of the TV show "Discovering."

After reaching the summit, we settled onto a rock outcrop on the north face of the ridge. Seated comfortably on a boulder, I went into my tale and recited the sequence of events from start to finish.

With the camera rolling the entire time, after about twenty minutes of nonstop blabber, I finally paused for long enough for the producer to holler "cuuut." After some rest for the arm holding the camera and a change of the battery, I continued on with the telling of the story. It was sort of a surreal experience, sitting there on that rock I had visited so many times, now telling my story into the eye of the camera. I looked around over the valley below me and to the mountains in the west, then turned my gaze to the shining sea in the distance. Cloudy as it was, it was a beautiful day.

November 23: The Food Truck

With the deer now fully processed and the cape delivered to the taxidermist, one of the last tasks to complete was to deliver some fresh venison to my friends. With a limited demand for meat in my house, once again I was happy to share with some friends who cherish the 100 percent organic steaks and roasts.

My first stop was to see my old friend Jim. He's the guy who, for years, did all of my professional photo processing. A magician in the darkroom, he used to razz me, calling me "the exposure doctor." Fortunately for me, he was often able to mask my occasional ineptitude in operating the camera with his skill in the darkroom making prints.

Old Jim was never a terribly skilled hunter, but he's always had a great taste for venison. Aside from its obvious health benefits, he just really enjoys the stuff. Once again, it was an honor to share a good portion of my deer with my old friend.

Perhaps the best part of my visit came when I asked Jim if he'd ever gotten a buck. Actually, he did get one many years ago. He turned and went to the back corner of the garage and returned with an old photo. It was a picture of a younger Jim, adorned in the typical clothing and hairstyle of a hipster in the early 1970s, smiling alongside a fat spike-horn buck.

"What's the story?" I asked.

"Well, Duane," Jim said, "I was at camp with some buddies over near Kenton. It was the first day of camp and we wanted a camp deer to feed the gang. So I walked out in the woods and sure enough, there was a deer. I didn't really care if it was a buck or not, so I just shot. And shot and shot.

"When the gun was empty and the deer was still standing there, I quickly reloaded and started shooting again. Eventually, I hit the deer and he went down. Well, when I got over there, I saw it was a little buck. Not really being prepared, I didn't have any rope. So I took off my outer layer of pants, tied them around his neck, and dragged him back to camp.

Sometimes, bucks can do dumb things when they're distracted by a doe in the picture.

"I kept going back to that camp for many years," Jim said, "and we always had a good time, but that was the only deer I ever shot. After a while, I found I was better at hunting deer with my Buick than I was with my gun."

In addition to appreciating his fun hunting story, I was happy to share the bounty of my harvest with my old friend. Happy too that I might prolong the life of his Buick's bumper, not to mention the life of some unsuspecting little roadside deer.

The next stop on my venison delivery route would be at my friend Brad's place. After having helped to haul the Legend out of the woods and load him into the truck, Brad was at the top of the priority list for prime cuts. Over the years, Brad had been a great hunting partner and still remains a great friend.

True to form, I found Brad still at work late that night. Once again, I told my big story, this time sharing the tale with Brad and his friend Mike. Still carrying my enthusiasm, I told the story with conviction, gesticulating freely in my animated recital. Every time I told the story, I took my audience along as I revisited the thrilling moments. And once again, I was thankful to have an interested audience.

To make the evening even more interesting, Brad and I shared a few more stories from our hunting experiences in seasons past. As we told his friend about big bucks who'd outsmarted us, we all shared a few laughs.

It's always fun to relive shared hunting memories with friends. I suppose reliving the memories has a tendency to keep the moments alive. Sort of like when we talk about an old friend or loved one who's gone, when we speak of them, they continue to live on. I suppose, it's better to live on only in memory than to not live on at all.

Because at the end of the day, when all the steps in the process have been completed, the memories are really all we're left with. The moments are gone and the future has yet to arrive. So we occupy the present with tales from our memories and hopes for the future.

Sharing the Bounty

In return for the venison quarters I shared with my friends, all I asked of them was that they saved the scraps for me after they carved the meat from the bones. My intent was to make full use of the animal I harvested. Even if I can't use certain parts, I know some other critter could. This in mind, I try to return whatever I can't use back to the wild. In doing so, I feel I allow parts of the animals I harvest to live on in the natural cycle of life.

My hope is, with every ounce of sustenance these fallen creatures provide to the carnivores of the world, a proportionate reduction in the burden of need will be relieved from the remaining living creatures. If those remains can help to feed the scavengers and predators, spare the life of another deer, or perhaps help feed an eagle for the season, I'm all for it.

After the shot area was removed, the last remains of the Legend were returned to the earth.

28 A SIDE STORY AND A MESSAGE

While it may be noble to share our excesses with others, I must share one note of caution. As providers of treats for the wild things, it's our duty to ensure that whatever we share is safe for those we share with. Specifically, I mention this because of a compelling experience I had in a previous season.

The day was November 29, 2010. After spending more than a week tracking a particular deer, I finally called off the chase. Feeling like I'd just done a marathon, I decided to spend a couple of hours riding the roads. Rolling through the pine-covered plains in the late morning, I spotted a deer, spooked and running toward the road in front of me. As he crossed the trail at full speed, I could see he was a decent buck.

Approaching his crossing, although the deer was long gone, I could tell by the track it was a mature buck. Wanting to give him a chance to settle down, I continued to the east, then took the next road south, to where he headed. Upon finding no exit tracks from that section of woods, I knew where he was and I knew he wasn't too far ahead. Knowing it was a good setup, I returned to his original crossing spot to take up the track.

With a few inches of fresh snow on top of a good base, the tracking was easy from the start. With no other fresh deer tracks around, there was no mistaking the path he chose. Moving at a steady clip through the dense stand of jack pine, the buck led me down a familiar secret path.

Pointing my toes into the powdery snow with each step, I was cruising with the silence of the wind. Having tracked a buck along this very same path several years ago, I knew the place well. As I approached a slight rise in the terrain, I remembered a favored bedding area among the aspens atop the knoll. Taking each step with caution, I picked the woods apart with my eyes, carefully searching for any glimpse of the deer I was expecting to see. As it turned out, the buck clearly had another destination in mind and passed quickly through the bedding area.

148

After following the spoor for a mile or more, we crossed the road at the southeast corner of the section with the buck maintaining his steady course to the southeast. At the road, I barely considered whether or not to continue with the track. I'd come this far and, now an hour into the track, I knew it wouldn't be long before the deer bedded down. Besides, he was headed straight for the canyon. I figured I'd keep with it till he made the canyon rim and if he dropped down, I'd drop out of the chase.

Transitioning from dense jack pines to the thick undergrowth of white pine and scrub oak, I had to slow my advance considerably in order to stay quiet. Picking my way through the brush as I doggedly followed the tracks, I cautiously approached a dense thicket of pine up ahead.

When I got to the point where the tracks took a hard turn to the left, I froze and looked around, again picking the woods apart inch by inch with my eyes. Unless he'd already bailed, he had to be right in front of me.

Although I was ready at every moment on the track, I was nonetheless startled when the deer jumped to his feet and broke cover a mere thirty yards ahead. Instantly I raised my gun, finger near the trigger, then watched as the buck bolted through two small openings in front of me. Looking over the iron sights, I could clearly see that the buck was a decent six-point, but not quite big enough to meet my standards. I held my fire.

It was a great hunt. And it was over. No sense in going any further chasing this deer. Maybe in a couple of years he'll be one to chase, but for now, it was time to move on. I wished him well and took great satisfaction in the conclusion of our cat-and-mouse match.

In the end we both won. I, in having successfully tracked him down to his lair, and he, in his mind at least, having outmaneuvered the hunter to live another day. With a smile, I began to make my retreat.

Returning to the road we'd recently crossed, I faced a seemingly insignificant decision. I could either take the easy way out and walk the road a mile or two back to the truck, or I could make my way cross-country and hunt my way back. While I was a little tired from the day's hiking, the decision was easy. With only a day and a half left in the season, the best hunting option was the only choice for me. Instead of taking the direct route back to where I came from, I decided to loop a mile or so to the west before heading back to the north.

Sneaking through the jack pines along the old and overgrown logging trails, I quietly made my way. As expected, there was little sign of life on this barren and frozen plain. Having traveled a mile west without finding a single fresh track, I turned north for the final leg of the journey. Following the contour of the old trail, I was happy to be out of the wind and among the shelter of the dense jack pine thicket. Rounding a gentle bend in the trail, I glanced down to the right and nearly jumped out of my skin.

Rounding a bend in the jack pines, I was startled by a strange creature at the base of a tree.

"HUUUH?" I spooked in mid-step and stumbled backward. Startled like when someone is hiding in the dark and jumps out in front of you with a surprising "boo," I'd swear my heart skipped a beat or two.

What the heck? What's that? My mind couldn't make sense of what I was seeing. There before me, less than three feet away, I spotted a medium-sized dark animal, hiding just behind the trunk of a stout jack pine. Whatever it was, it was close enough that it could have gotten my leg in one little leap.

What is it? I looked closer. Partially covered by the fresh dusting of snow, I saw … feathers? It took a moment to register what I was seeing.

No, I thought. It can't be. After a few moments, when I detected no movement and my heart settled back to its normal rhythm, I took a step forward and poked the critter with the muzzle of my rifle. Nothing. Again, I poked, and again, no movement. I reached down, brushed away the snow and revealed her majesty.

It was feathers, all right. I'd found an unimaginable find. The king or queen of the sky, it was none other than an adult bald eagle. Bending down, I pried the bird up and out of its snowy resting place at the base of the tree. Unfortunately for the magnificent eagle, she was partly stiff, cold as a stone and dead as a doornail. I turned the bird on its back and took a closer look. Its bright yellow beak and feet stood in sharp contrast to its dark main plumage. Also standing out was the size of its head and the parrot-like beak.

Perhaps most amazing was the fact that, when I picked the bird up, it was perfectly intact without so much as a single feather missing. With the prosperous canine population in the area, it was obvious the eagle had died very recently. The recent passing of the bird was confirmed when I grasped a wing in each hand and spread the bird's glorious wings.

It was so fresh, any signs of decomposition or rigor-mortis had yet to set in. Indeed it was a perfect specimen. I sat with the eagle for more than an hour, admiring its beauty and trying to imagine the life it had lived. After some quiet contemplation, I spoke to the trees and the wind, asking that the eagle rest in peace and that its spirit would fly on.

Before moving on, I spent another hour taking photos of the spectacular specimen. At the conclusion of the photo session I carefully wrapped the bird in a blanket and tucked it into the truck for the ride home.

On the way home I stopped at my friend Mike's camp to share the story. As I awaited his return from the woods, just after dark he pulled up with his nephew, Christian. Ironically enough, earlier in the evening while I was sitting with the eagle, Mike was helping his nephew get his first buck, a nice seven-pointer. Needless to say, it was an eventful night for storytelling at the old camp and one we'll long remember.

Upon arriving home, I brought the bird up to the house and out on the deck. I spread its wings and showed the wife. It was mesmerizing to be in the presence of such a magnificent creature. As we closely examined the fallen fowl, we were nearly speechless.

The next day I called the Michigan DNR in Marquette and made arrangements to bring the bird in. Upon arrival at the DNR field office, the biologist examined the bird for any signs of trauma.

With a wingspan of nearly seven feet, surprisingly, the eagle seemed to be light as a feather.

Touching a bald eagle and seeing one up close is a mesmerizing experience.

After finding no sign of injury or an obvious cause of death, the eagle was sent to the DNR laboratory in Lansing for a thorough necropsy. A few weeks later, I got the results. According to the biologists at the DNR lab, the eagle was an adult female of approximately five years of age. The bird was found to be in a severely emaciated state. Further analysis of the stomach contents revealed the eagle died from acute lead poisoning.

As it turns out, lead poisoning is one of the leading causes of death among bald eagles across North America. As hunters, we're likely responsible for the majority of the lead that enters our environment and kills our eagles.

How does an eagle get lead poisoning? Being opportunistic feeders, eagles often ingest lead fragments while scavenging on the remains of animals harvested by hunters or by feeding on unretrieved carcasses and pest animals killed with lead ammunition. And it doesn't take much lead to do-in an eagle. For a bird that weighs seven to fourteen pounds, an amount of lead as small as a grain of rice is enough to kill three adult bald eagles.

According to a report published in 2014 by the National Wildlife Health Center (part of the U.S. Geological Survey), of 2,980 bald eagles examined between 1982 and 2013, the leading causes of death were poisoning (26 percent) followed by trauma (23 percent). Of those that died by poisoning, 64 percent were confirmed to have succumbed to lead poisoning.

In my experience, on numerous occasions, I believe I've observed one of the most common sources of lead poisoning in eagles. You don't have to drive too far in the backwoods of the U.P. to find the remains of butchered deer along the sides of the trails. Often, these bone piles will be revealed by a group of ravens and eagles that jump up from their feast as you drive by.

Now, it's legal, sort of, to leave the remains of harvested animals in the woods, for bait or otherwise. The problem lies in what we leave behind. Usually, hunters will leave anything that's not fit for human consumption. And this often includes the part of the animal that took the brunt of the shot. With a good shoulder shot on a deer, a soft-point lead bullet will shatter and fragment into tiny pieces at the point of impact.

So when a person leaves those shot-up parts of a carcass out for the critters, he's often leaving behind a deadly batch of lead fragments. With this in mind, I strongly urge all hunters who still use lead ammo to be sure to properly dispose of any parts of hunted animals that could contain lead fragments. If everyone would make the effort to clean up their scraps, we could probably save a few eagles.

Better yet, I encourage anyone who participates in shooting sports to consider making the switch to lead-free ammunition. Other viable options do exist. While I wasn't able to find any copper-solid ammo locally, I was able to order some over the phone. For a little more than $25, my box of twenty rounds arrived within a few days. While copper ammo costs just a little more than lead, to me it's worth the cost if it helps protect the lives of eagles and the health of our environment.

Each year, several hundred million rounds of lead ammunition are fired off in North America, releasing thousands of tons of lead into the environment. This highly toxic metal adversely affects the nervous and reproductive systems of humans and often causes death in wildlife.

In 1991, the use of lead shot was banned in waterfowl hunting. While the law has helped protect waterfowl and waterways, studies have shown that lead poisoning continues to be a leading cause of mortality for bald eagles.

It's not only bald eagles that are suffering. Other studies have shown that raptors and scavengers around the world are highly susceptible to lead poisoning. And with the sublethal effects of lead toxicity often going undetected, the overall impact of lead poisoning in wildlife is probably vastly underestimated.

In areas where experiments have been undertaken to replace lead ammunition with non-lead ammunition for hunting, studies indicate that the ingestion of lead by bald eagles has declined significantly.

The sad truth is, the lead we hunters leave behind continues to cause harm among wildlife populations. Maybe it's time to take our laws a step further and eliminate the use of lead ammunition for all hunting.

Perhaps the story of this eagle's death will help prevent future fatalities from lead poisoning.

To me, it was a spiritual experience finding that eagle. Of all the paths I could have chosen, something guided my steps to that time and place. In that moment and still to this day, I feel a connection to the spirit of the eagle. Knowing how it died, it almost feels like it was put in my path so I could share its message. And the message is this: We humans can and should take steps to protect the lives of eagles and other wildlife.

With only photos and memories of the eagle remaining, the best I can do now is share her story. Perhaps with the knowledge of this eagle's death, we can be inspired to take bold steps to do more to prevent our lead from contaminating the environment and entering the digestive tracts of eagles.

For now, I'm not waiting for the laws to change. It's sort of like catching a female fish who's in the act of spawning, then choosing to release it. Even if it's legal to keep the fish, releasing it is usually the right thing to do.

This year, in my .30-06, I'll be shooting 150 grain copper-solid bullets made by Winchester. My old friend Bob at the local sporting goods store told me it'll perform well, with better weight retention, more expansion, and better wound channeling than traditional lead ammo.

After finding an eagle who had fallen to lead poisoning, research taught me lead ammo was leading to widespread problems among wildlife. Further research taught me that lead-free bullets are available. Now, the writing is on the wall. In the future, I'll be using lead-free ammunition.

29 RETURNING TO THE WOODS

November 24: A Tale Told in the Tracks

After eight straight days spent at home dealing with the Legend, the work was finally done. It was time to return to the woods. Not really concerned with harvesting another deer, I left home at the leisurely hour of 1 p.m. Under cloudy skies with temperatures in the upper thirties and with a few inches of slushy melting snow, it would have been a fine day for a hunt.

Fortunately for the deer in my neck of the woods, my hunting was all but done. While I had no intention of harvesting another animal, that old magnetic pull that draws me to the woods each autumn still had its grip on me. Regardless of my conscious lack of desire to kill, my subconscious beckoned me to get back in the woods. Likewise, my curiosity had me wondering what was happening in my favorite old haunts.

With a shortened day to work with after returning the Legend's remains to the woods, I returned to a favorite place where multiple runways cross, a spot where mature bucks annually stake out their territorial claims. Sneaking up the trail toward the top of the ridge, I was following a good set of buck tracks that were laid down within the past twenty-four hours.

Reaching the crest of the hill, I paused at a fresh scrape in the middle of the trail. With fresh dirt strewn about on top of the snow, it looked like this deer had gone partially berserk in making his scrape. Strangely, it wasn't just the scrape that was all torn up. Instead, an area the size of my dining room was all churned up as if a small rodeo had just taken place there.

A closer look revealed another set of buck tracks coming up the ridge from the other direction. And there in the middle of the snowy trail, the bucks' trails converged. Surveying the scene, it was obvious these two bucks happened to arrive at the same place at the same time, and the result was anything but cordial.

A great buck battle broke out near here, where two trails cross at the crest of the ridge.

Rather, it was clear this meeting was contentious, to say the least. Apparently, both of these fellows seemed to believe they had a rightful claim to the territory. When diplomatic channels broke down, it appears a brawl was quick to break out. With that slushy snow telling the tale of the tangle, it was obvious what had gone down. And it was unlike anything I had ever seen.

There before me lay the telltale signs of an extended buck battle. And this was no casual sparring match. The dispute broke out over the scrape and extended out from there. The first round of the brawl involved some pushing and shoving in a circular area immediately adjacent to the scrape.

Judging by the tracks in the snow, the two mature bucks then found their antlers locked together. From there, the battle extended down the ridge and on through the dense vegetation of the secondary growth forest. It was as if two bulls had been locked in battle, tied together at the head, and were pushing, pulling, kicking, and scratching their way along. With elbow and knee marks driven deep into the dirt and clods of soil strewn about, those bucks tore that little hillside apart. Crashing down the hill in a rotating radius as broad as the lengths of two deer, the path of destruction was extensive and thorough.

Breaking branches and plowing down trees as big around as my arm and ten feet tall, the battle line was marked with torn-up turf, tufts of hair, and toppled trees. It looked like two Tasmanian devils had just whirled their wild way through.

Following this path of destruction, I could barely believe what was unfolding before my eyes. Taking my time on the trail, I tightened my grip on my rifle as I looked ahead for the combatants. Scanning the woods with my eyes, my feet cautiously moved forward. The whole time my mind raced, wondering what I might find up ahead.

Now, we've all heard stories about an unsuspecting hunter stumbling upon two antler-stuck trophy bucks, and that's just where my trail appeared to be headed. Projecting my thinking out to the end game, I wasn't quite sure where to go with this. What if I find those two big bucks locked together? With only one tag left, shooting both bucks would not be an option. For that matter, I didn't even want to shoot one of those bucks. I already had my supply of venison for the year and to take any more would be gluttonous. Not sure what I would do if I found them, I followed the tracks anyway.

Pausing to scan the woods ahead, I thought about what I was into now. It seemed impossible. After having just completed my hunt of a lifetime, here I was, my very next time out in the woods, and I was fast onto the trail of two big bucks locked together in battle. It was a sight I'd never seen, a scenario I had occasionally imagined, and the scene of any hunter's dreams. My heart raced. With each step, I fully expected to see those bucks at any moment. Deep down, I was just hoping to get some photos and video, secretly hoping to perhaps release those bucks from their death trap.

Continuing down the trail of battle, the bucks came alongside a huge white pine that had recently fallen. Now it appeared that one of the combatants was starting to get the upper hand. It looked like the one deer had been momentarily pinned against that giant tree, leaving large clumps of rump hair on the sharp stubs where the branches had broken from the trunk.

Emerging from the white pine battle cage, the bucks remained locked together and began tussling their way back up the ridge and to the south. Crashing through a dense thicket of balsam and pine, the battle trail crested the ridge, and began to drop into another dense stand of balsam. Getting close now, I was fully expecting to find them just up ahead.

Passing the massive stump of the giant fallen pine, the battle trail came to an abrupt halt at a wall of evergreens. As quickly as it began, it was over. After more than 100 yards of destruction, the trail of tribulation ended with the tracks of two deer running away, with the victor chasing the loser for about thirty yards before peeling off in his own direction.

Finding the evidence of their escape, I was relieved they'd solved the matter on their own and without the need for my intervention. I paused for a few moments and wondered at the miracle of life in the forest and my incredible good luck in forest foraging. For the moment, I was happy to simply be a witness to the workings of the wild world.

November 25: A Broken Silence

For this day, I took a ride up to an old friend's camp at the far edge of the county. He wasn't able to make it for the season and had asked me to check on his place. Cruising the trails in the vicinity of his camp, I saw an eagle, spotted some moose and wolf tracks, found just a few deer tracks, and saw few other vehicles. It all looked good, with more sign of wildlife than human life. Then I parked the truck for a hike into the hills.

Finding a feeder creek to muffle the sounds of my steps, I made my way up the face of the rocky ridge, climbing higher and higher toward the oak plateau above. On a small scale, looking down at the mossy ground, for all I knew, I may have been the only man to ever step foot here. On a larger scale, as I looked around I could see the evidence of a logging operation that had thinned the hillside canopy some decades ago.

Okay, so maybe no one had set foot here in a decade or two. In the intervening years, the earth was healing its wounds and returning to its natural state. At least for today, I was all alone in a wild and wonderful world unspoiled by the development of mankind.

Except, unfortunately, I wasn't alone at all. Rather, my unseen companion for the day was just the thing I had come here to escape. Like a nuisance that won't go away, the drone of humanity buzzed incessantly in my ear.

A foreign invader in a land of tranquility, it was the never-ending buzz of a bee that wouldn't bug off. Try as I might, I couldn't ignore it. The peaceful silence was broken. It was the unsettling sound of industry. And its incessant drone drowned out the sounds of trickling rivulets and filled the forest airways with sounds of the city.

Reaching the crest of the hill, I turned to look out over the valley from which I had just ascended. Below, a vast plain spread out before me, wooded and wild as far as the eyes could see. With one small exception. There, about a mile away, I could see the structures of a new industrial development.

Now, I understand we need industry to provide things we need. But here in this otherwise silent space, the sounds of heavy equipment delving forward and beeping backward was akin to a disorderly drunk at the Sunday service. The sounds of man interrupted the silence and spoiled the solitude otherwise found in a long-forgotten corner of the forest. So foreign was the sound, I could hardly focus on the moment, nor could I become one with the natural surroundings.

I tried to hike the hills, tried to get away from the awful sound. However, no matter where I went, the droning of engines and thunder of heavy equipment persisted. I found myself so distracted by the din, my only choice was to descend the hill and retreat to a quieter corner of the county.

Even in the deepest of woods, the sense of solitude can be ruined by sounds of civilization.

Having heard enough, I had to get away as soon as possible. I'd gone there to escape city sounds. So you can understand my frustration when I went to this previously silent spot, miles from civilization, only to discover the sounds of the city had taken over. It was disappointing to say the least.

As you can probably tell by now, I hunt for more than deer when deer hunting. Chief among the things I seek is peace and quiet. To that end, I go to great lengths to put myself in those rare places where you hear not a plane, train, nor automobile. In a world where mankind has left his mark just about everywhere, I try to find the few places that remain virtually untouched by the hands of people.

Even though it looked the same, the place was different now. The song of the forest with the wind in the pines had been muted by the hubbub of humanity. Although it had long been one of my favorite places, I knew I had to move on. The area still had deer, but you can find deer anywhere. To find the things I was seeking, I would have to look elsewhere.

30 WALKING IN THE STEPS OF A LEGEND

November 26

For dinner the previous night, I cooked some of the fresh venison. Cooked in the pan with some butter and fresh vegetables and served on a bed of brown rice and with a potato and carrots on the side, it was a meal fit for a king. Not only that, it was as healthy a meal as could be found anywhere. I savored the delicious nourishment. And with that, the Legend had become a part of me.

With the Legend now seeing through my eyes, we walked together through his old haunts. Our first stop was the place of his passing, where we memorialized the occasion with some light carvings on a tree.

From there, we continued on the path to where he was headed on his fateful last day. We proceeded on to where he would have gone had I not been there to intervene. Walking slowly, observing the scrapes he carefully tended and touching the rubs on the trees he'd savagely marked, I felt a pit in my stomach. It was like that feeling you get when you lose a loved one. My old friend was gone and there was nothing I could do to change it.

And yet, walking the trails through his former forest kingdom, I could sense the shadow of his presence. These were his trails and since he was gone, the woods seemed almost vacant. No fresh tracks in the dirt, no activity at his scrapes. Instead, everywhere I looked I saw the afterimage of the last time the Legend passed this way.

I spent the day hiking along his network of trails through miles of rugged forest. The feeling of sadness never left the pit of my stomach. And everywhere I looked, I saw the ghost of the Legend. While I saw no sign of any other bucks daring to tread on the Legend's main turf, I did see a single deer on a small peak in the next range of mountains to the east.

Once a signpost on the Legend's trail, I carried this one home to stand in the man-cave.

The young buck had a perfect perch in the dense pines that topped the hill. Like he must have done many times before, when he heard me approach from the northeast, he keenly dropped off the back of the ridge and down to the northwest. Surely this buck was an acquaintance of the Legend. Perhaps he'd be the next in line to the throne of Thunder Canyon. If so, he would soon lay claim to one of the finest patches of forest ever found in the north woods.

Continuing my survey of the Legend's turf, I turned back to the north and headed for the northeast parcel of his kingdom. Along the way, I cut down a couple of his rubs and brought them along for the ride. I figured they'd make good walking sticks or simply serve as souvenirs.

Either way, I brought them along. The impressive rubs had left the trees completely girdled and doomed to certain death. Rather than leave them to rot, I brought them home so the Legend could be surrounded by some of his chosen trees. It just seemed like the right thing to do.

November 27 to 30

For the last few days of the season I wandered, waking well after prime-time and arriving late to no particular destination. I drove around a little checking the countryside and walked a lot, exploring territory old and new. It was still open season and I still had a license to hunt. What I didn't have was an inkling of desire to kill another deer.

Walking in the land of the Legend, the forest seemed to stand still in his absence.

I don't remember exactly where I went or what I did those last few days. All I really recall is hiking mile after mile in the deep woods the Legend once called home. Where once I had an intense drive to compete, I was left only with the desire to observe. Soaking up the sights and smells and sounds with my senses opened wide, after a few days, I felt like the forest had become a part of me and I'd become a part of the forest. It was comforting, yet discomforting at the same time.

Exceptionally quiet, the world of the woods seemed empty without the Legend. A thread of sadness tugged at my heart. In claiming my ultimate victory, I had ended the life of the creature I revered. Strangely, no longer did I feel the thrill of victory. Rather, I found myself more in a state of mourning.

Although I'd achieved a goal of a lifetime, after the race was over, I felt a little different than I might have expected. Maybe it was out of respect for the opponent or perhaps it was because I knew it was over. Whatever it was, something seemed to subdue the feeling of satisfaction.

31 LOOKING FORWARD, LOOKING BACK

It almost seems like it was too easy. It was only the second day of the season and by the time the sun had risen, my season had come to a close. Unlike past seasons when I'd logged days and weeks of efforts, hiked for miles upon miles, and waited for hours on end, this season I had barely gotten started. In finding that perfect moment of convergence, it all seemed so simple. Except it wasn't.

In reality, recalling all I'd endured over the past three years in my quest for the Legend, and indeed over the past thirty years, it was unquestionably the most difficult challenge I'd ever participated in. Through years of grueling effort I faced many tough days. I'd shed a little blood, a lot of sweat, twenty pounds, and a few tears along the way. I was rained on, snowed upon, and stuck in the mud. I'd been defeated, exhausted, and wanted to pull the plug. But through it all, I heard the call, and never quit until I saw the buck fall.

It was similar in scope to my earning accolades as a state champion athlete as a youth and navigating the path through college as a young adult. All of which required a vision, a goal, a huge commitment of time, a relentless commitment to excellence, years of dedication, intense desire, a strong will, and the persistence to follow through to the very end.

Except this was even more difficult than those other quests, because this time, the target was always on the move. It was a true test of spirit. Ultra demanding both physically and mentally, my quest required persistence and dedication, dogged determination, and a relentless pursuit of perfection. In good weather and poor, whether I wanted to or not, I was in constant training for a marathon with no known finish line. In order to find that finish line, I had to transform myself to an iron-willed wolf-man.

Finding a big buck in the U.P. wilderness sometimes takes years of effort.

Eventually I found that finish line, and when I crossed over I lifted my chin and howled at the setting super-moon. Not wanting to give my stealthy self away, it was a somewhat stifled howl. And though it was quelled, never had there been a more heartfelt howl. It was at once a cry of joy and a bawl of sadness. And it was a statement about all that had led to the moment. A battle cry of sorts, it spoke of my hard-earned victory as much as my respect for my fallen comrade.

Along the course of my quest, I found good times and bad, success and failure, and memories to last a lifetime. I lived amazing stories, found incredible treasures, and took some nice photos. But perhaps the most important things I take away are the lessons learned. Sure, I learned some things about deer hunting. And that would be great for a guy who has a lifetime of hunting ahead. But for me, some of the most important things I learned were related to the value of wildlife and wild places.

Looking forward, it's tough to see where to go. When the mission is accomplished and you reach the pinnacle of success, what comes next? It would seem to be a simple question, but the truth is, it's a complicated set of questions. Do I seek the next adventure or do I sit back and reflect on adventures past? Am I satisfied with my accomplishments or do I thirst for more? Do I return for another season or do I hang it up? Do I strive to do more? Or do I simply quit while I'm ahead?

While I'm not sure what the future holds, I do hope to have many more adventures while hunting, regardless of whether I pull the trigger or not.

Like most hunters these days, I hunt not necessarily because I need the meat, but more because it's my chance to connect with the natural world. When hunting, I can leave the civilized world behind, interact with the wild creatures of the wilderness, and listen to the sounds of silence. It's my opportunity to live for a moment in the old way, when it was simply a daily quest to survive. I can listen to the wind and watch the wild world as it goes about its business in the way it has for thousands of generations.

There's just something soothing about being on forest time, where it's either daytime or nighttime. The only demands in forest time are to find food, water, and enough shelter to refresh oneself with a few hours of rest. And though there may be times of difficulty and stress, the overarching aura of the hunter in the woods is a state of peaceful and simple existence, in a natural place where the masses of humanity have yet to encroach.

Ultimately, most of us just want to get away from the trappings of everyday life in the civilized world. After being stuck so long on the inside and shackled to the responsibilities of modern life, all we really want is to feel alive and free. So we go hunting.

As for me, looking back I recall the difficulties associated with hunting for the Legend. I remember the excitement and frustration during the process, then the thrill and sadness at the conclusion. The aftertaste is bittersweet. As much as I enjoy the hunting, as much as I enjoy a meal of roasted vegetables and venison, I've learned that the best parts of hunting don't usually involve the actual harvest of game.

Seeing wildlife and connecting with the wild world is reason enough to hunt.

32 THE TRUE MEASURE OF SUCCESS

Whether we're hunting, fishing, working, or playing, ultimately the goal is to achieve some degree of success. In work, we want to do well and earn our pay. In most games, the object is to win. Likewise, when we fish, we hope to catch fish. And when we hunt, usually the underlying goal is to get that which we hunt for. But it's not that simple.

In whatever we do, it's important to remember that the Olympic medals are available only once every four years. In other words, the opportunity to claim the ultimate prize doesn't come along every day. In fact, most days on the road to glory are rather mundane.

In order to walk the road to success, one must build that road first. And as any roughneck knows, the business of road building can be hard work. First there's the planning. Then it's the blood, sweat, and tears of the heavy lifting. After the tedious finishing touches, the day comes when the ribbon is cut and the project is deemed a success.

Was the project a success only on the day of completion? Of course not. In reality, the successful completion of the project is built upon multiple layers of many successes. Along the way, there will be bad days and failures. But in the grand scheme, each day that's dedicated to the completion of a project is one of many small successes that lead to big success.

So it goes with hunting. If we only measured our success by the weight of our harvest each day, most of our days would be deemed unsuccessful. And who wants to keep failure as a regular companion? Sure, we hope to get that buck sooner or later, but we have to remember, like with anything else, achieving success is a process. And that process includes many layers of effort before the project is complete.

In my case, it took many years of effort and many moments of failure in order to build and walk upon my road to the ultimate success.

Success was found on this day when I spotted a friendly woods-chicken. Protected from hunting in Michigan since 1914, the spruce grouse is mostly unafraid of curious humans.

The great thing about hunting is, even on the days of our greatest failures, we can reap some measure of success when we consider the scope of the bigger picture. A failure today may eventually be considered a success when it becomes a critical lesson leading to our larger success of tomorrow.

Larger success aside, most people who hunt do it for more than just the meat. We do it for the thrill of the chase. Perhaps more than that, we do it to connect with the natural world and our tribe. Of course it'd be much easier to buy our meat at the supermarket, but that's not what it's about. It's about living life the old way, in the old world, where animals and waters still run free. We go hunting to get away from the modern world and back to a more natural state. And if not that, we go to hunting camp to spend time with our people in the old way, away from the trappings, technology, and distractions of modern everyday life.

Because of our deep-rooted desire to be free and natural, it's easy to find and claim success, even after the worst days of hunting. If you're doing it for the right reasons, even on the days when you see not a hair, you have achieved success simply by being there. After all, how can it be a bad day if it's a day spent in the woods or at camp with your crew. This optimistic outlook has to be embraced if you want to have a long and successful hunting career.

Hunting success is a lot like happiness: It can be found anywhere. It's all a matter of how you look at it. Enter the game with a positive attitude, end the game with a positive result.

33 INTO THE FUTURE

If I wanted to follow the advice of the masses who recommend you should quit while you're ahead, this would've been the perfect time to walk away. Having achieved my ultimate goal as a hunter, thoughts of retirement started to surface. As the 2017 season approached, I seriously wondered what I would do when the new season arrived.

I wasn't sure I'd ever hunt again after the year of the Legend. My appetite to kill was all but gone, and my will to work hard for a hunt was nearly nonexistent. I had reached the pinnacle of hunting success, and I was satisfied with all I'd done in my hunting career.

And yet a yearning to return to the woods grew as the leaves left the trees. It was a primal calling, the light of the hunter's moon having stirred a movement deep inside. As it had for the past thirty years, my instinct called me back to the woods.

Perhaps my hunting career should have come to a close in 2016. But, of course, it didn't. As the 2017 season drew closer, my desire to renew the hunt grew stronger and I knew I'd get back in the game. Whatever might happen, in the year after I'd reached the top, I wondered how the story might continue. Or how it might conclude.

I still wasn't sure what I'd do in the moment of truth, but there was no doubt the old yearning to walk the forest was alive and well. Regardless of whether or not I wanted to harvest any game, I was certain I wanted to hunt again. If only to feel the breeze and see the forest, my thirst to escape to the wild world was as strong as ever.

With a few weeks remaining before the 2017 season, I took a hike through the land of the Legend, looking for sign and scouting. From the moment I arrived, I knew this season would be different. The bulldozers had come in and, where once there was an overgrown two-track trail, there now was a fully graded, double-wide logging road.

Shortly after the bulldozers invaded my secret spot, the lumberjacks arrived to cut the trees.

How ironic. One year I find the holy land of the hunt and the next year the land is leveled by bulldozers. I continued with the hike, walking through the barely recognizable land of the Legend. Not surprisingly, there was very little deer sign in the area and zero buck sign to be found.

The lumberjacks had landed, and their target was the very trees under which the Legend had walked. That trail I had tiptoed down and subsequently toiled upon to haul the Legend out was now a forest freeway, opened up to all the traffic of the woods.

Worse yet, the old trail where the Legend had maintained his extensive scrape-line had now been transformed into a regular road, passing within 50 yards of where I sat and where the Legend had fallen.

There would be no encore performance on this stage. The theater was demolished and the actors had moved on. Although the deer will come back someday, it'll be decades before the place looks like it did. Without much choice, I too had to move on.

They say when one door closes, another one opens – that endings lead to new beginnings. Always welcoming a new adventure, I eagerly embraced the challenges that came with the changes. And with the spirit of a young explorer, I boldly turned the page and set my course into the unknown. Wherever my path might lead, I was excited to embark upon my next wilderness adventures.

After the Fall of the Legend

When the 2017 season arrived, I was back at it. The deer had shifted their patterns a bit and I'd adjusted my plans. Like previous seasons, I spent a good amount of time in the woods. But unlike years past, I lacked the will to work very hard. Having achieved my big goal as a hunter in 2016, the 2017 season was more of a casual experience.

As it turns out, the 2017 season was interesting to say the least. Did I find success? Absolutely. Was it the usual, same old story? Far from it. But like all hunting seasons, it was a fun season filled with surprising stories, unexpected turns, and lessons learned. In the end, the 2017 season ended up being funnier than it was fatal. And that was quite all right.

To make a long story short, I tried some different techniques and in the process played cat and mouse with several little bucks, but never saw a big buck. The highlight of my 2017 season came on the last day when two decent bucks crossed at less than thirty yards, grunting the whole way as they chased a hot doe. How it all went down is a long story for another day. For now, it's safe to say the season ended in a draw. I passed up plenty of smaller bucks and was certain there'd be bigger bucks to hunt next year.

The only thing I was left wondering was what I'd do the next time I got a chance at a big buck. Along with that, I wondered how long I'd have to wait to find the answer. I just hoped it wouldn't take another thirty years before my next encounter with a legend-sized buck.

On the last day of the 2017 season, I passed on this buck before he visited my camera trap.

The Tradition Continues

Going into the 2018 hunting season, I was looking forward to the annual renewal of my rivalry with the bucks of Thunder Canyon. Having watched a nice eight-pointer walk away on the last day of the previous season, I was eager to see how the new season might unfold.

As is often the case, the days of autumn blew past like leaves in the wind, and before I knew it, October had slipped away. Running out of time to do everything, I decided to focus on the top priorities. And since the fall of the Legend, my priorities had changed somewhat. This year, it seemed most important to spend more quality time hunting with my old dad.

With this in mind, instead of scouting my spots close to home, I decided to spend my free time traveling to our southern Michigan farm for the annual archery and camera hunt with Dad. As it turns out, our three-day adventure in early November led to my next encounter with a buck of legendary proportions. More importantly, the time spent with Dad evolved into one of the most satisfying stories of my hunting career.

The farm covers nearly 100 acres of fertile soil, situated about thirty miles south of Lansing. When Dad bought the place in '78, it was mostly open fields with a few moist swales, some wooded fencerows, and a couple of oak woodlots. Through the decades, as we grew we watched the land grow.

But it was more than idle observation. Because over the course of thirty some years, Dad planted thousands of trees on the spread in order to create the perfect deer habitat. It started with dozens of apple trees, continued with hundreds of scotch pines, and continued further with thousands of white pines, spruces, and oaks. Now forty years later, the investment has matured, and under the shade of the young forest the wildlife abounds in a perfectly planned community.

With trees planted in strategic locations to provide food, shelter, sanctuary, and travel corridors for the deer, the farm has evolved into a deer hunter's dreamland. With multiple rows of pines bordering the perimeter and several crop fields protected in the core, the property offers everything a deer might want for a long and prosperous life.

The farm also offers everything a hunter could hope for. Having hunted the place for forty years, we have a pretty good idea what the deer like to do and when. Accordingly, we've got dozens of stands set up at key locations, plus we have walking trails cleared for easy access.

Needless to say, for a hunter who does most of his hunting alone in the toughest of terrain of the Upper Peninsula, to venture south to a true hunting haven is a real treat. While I love the wild aspects of the U.P., it's always exciting to head south for a couple of days of farmland hunting with my favorite old hunting partner. Not only would it be nice to spend some time with Dad, but it would also be fun to finally see lots of deer.

There's always a chance you'll see a big buck in farm country. This one showed up in 2013.

The season started on Friday, November 1 when I left home just after midnight. After driving seven hours through the night, I met Dad at the ranch. A few minutes before first light we proceeded to our stands. I'd been cooking up my plans for weeks, thinking about strategies, where to go and when. For the first hunt, Dad went to one of his favorite stands near the big field and I went to a new stand we'd set in the pines to the north.

I arrived at my spot just before daylight. At first light my plan proved to be good as a buck approached to twenty yards. Still early, I couldn't see his rack but I could tell he was a big deer. As he entered a small clearing, he caught a whiff of me then stood on alert for a long time as the light developed. As it got lighter, I could see he was about a fourteen-inch, two-year-old eight-point.

Finally, when there was enough light to see clearly, he reversed course and went back where he came from. Unfortunately for me, it was still too dark for the camera and he got away before I could get a shot. A few minutes later, we talked on the radio and I told Dad to keep an eye out as the buck was headed his way.

Sure enough, the deer went by him a little while later and offered a good shot opportunity. Unfortunately for old Dad, he was unable to draw his bow in the moment of truth. He could draw the bow just fine standing on the ground before the hunt, but perched in a rather small ladderstand, he didn't want to risk his safety by standing up. And he couldn't draw from a seated position. Though he was disappointed, he was still a happy hunter.

All in all it was a good hunt. The plan was good. The deer just got lucky.

Friday afternoon, we skipped the hunt and went to see a great high school football game. I was so stoked after watching my nephews lead their team to its first championship in school history, I could barely sleep that night.

After just a couple hours of sleep, we were up and at 'em early Saturday. This time, the plan was to have Dad go to the north narrows stand and I'd go to the southwest brushy field, not far from where I tagged Mr. B.G. in 1986. Right away I had a little buck go right under me. A while later another little guy came by and I got a couple shots of him.

At around 9, I heard a snort to the northwest, then awhile later, another. With the wind blowing out of the southeast, I figured they smelled me. Looking behind me toward the source of the snort, I didn't see anything. Then I heard another snort. Wanting a better view, I shifted sidesaddle on the stand so I could see the green field where the sound was coming from.

Within a few minutes chaos broke loose and there was group of deer running around the field. With several bucks chasing a lone doe, it looked like a wild ring-around-the-rosy. After a few circles the doe ran from the field and into the woods, right underneath me. Here comes the parade. A small buck followed the doe, then another little guy followed suit. And just that quick, all the deer disappeared to the east and into the brushy field.

I shifted back to center, facing east on the ladderstand and looked for more activity. In a few minutes, I detected movement out of the corner of my eye and looked to the north. Right away I could see it was a big buck.

"Holy cow. It's a whopper. And he's coming right at me."

Here he comes. The day was November 2, 2018, and it was a buck of legendary proportions.

173

Since 1996 when I began my photography career, I've always carried a camera while hunting. Whether hunting with a bow and arrow or firearm, during the past twenty-two seasons more than ninety percent of the deer I've shot have been with the camera. Through the years, I've found that hunting with the camera can be just as challenging and is often even more satisfying than hunting with projectiles.

If you've ever missed or wounded a big buck, you know how it feels. It's a sickening feeling, to work so hard for something, only to blow it in the moment of truth. Hunting with the camera is different. You'll never have to feel bad about killing or wounding a beautiful animal. And if you do screw up the first shot opportunity, usually you'll get another chance. At worst, you'll get an out-of-focus or underexposed image. But most of the time, you go home with at least something, and usually it's the feeling of success.

Sitting in a tree less than a hundred yards from where Mr. B.G. fell thirty-two years ago, and only a couple of seasons removed from the season of The Legend, this time my wait was less than two years before I spotted another legendary buck approaching.

Unlike that day in 1986 when I was armed only with a gun, or the day in 2016 when I was on a mission, this time I had a choice. Without a split second of second thought, I reached past the bow hanging on the tree beside me and grabbed the camera. While it looked to be a buck as big as or bigger than the Legend, I had no intention of making an attempt to take his life. At this point, it was thrilling enough just to see another huge buck.

Trying to manually focus through the tangle of trees, I snapped a few shots as he approached. After a couple of stops along the way to check the wind, the big buck proceeded to walk right past me, offering a perfect quartering away shot at about seventeen yards.

Although he was walking pretty steady and wasting no time in looking for that hot doe, I managed to take 5 shots in the five steps he took at close range before he ducked into the spruces. While my shots weren't perfect, I knew I got a couple of good ones.

As the huge buck disappeared into the dense stand of spruces, adrenalin still coursed through my veins. I got my buck, the thrill was to the core, and this time, there was no remorse. It was just as I wanted it. One of the biggest bucks I'd ever seen while hunting, I was proud to let him go. The best part was, this time, we both won.

In the moments after the big buck walked away, I savored the moment and thought about my hunting career. After thirty-five years of hunting, I'd come full circle. Where once I was shaking with anticipation, hoping to get my biggest buck ever, this time I was shaking with excitement, having chosen to let one of the biggest bucks I'd ever seen live to see another day.

Completely unaware of my presence, the massive buck offered a perfect shot opportunity.

At around 9:30, Dad and I talked on the radio. I shared the news of my great hunt, then he shared his report. Turns out, he also had a big buck offer a good shot opportunity. This time, he was able to get the bow drawn and was about to take a shot. Unfortunately, as he was preparing to take aim, his finger prematurely bumped the trigger sending his arrow woefully short and into the dirt.

While he was happy for my success, Dad was somewhat frustrated with his results. I encouraged him to hang in there. It was still early, I told him, the deer were still on the move. I really believed he'd get another chance.

Just after 10 a.m. Dad called again to give me the latest update.

"I think I just got my big buck," he whispered into the radio.

"You're kiddin me," I said. "Tell me what happened."

Through the radio, he told his story. As the big buck approached, still frustrated with his previous results, Dad decided to try something he was certain he *could* do. So he got his camera ready. His little point-and-shoot cheapo camera, to be precise. I was thrilled to hear him tell how he got several good shots, but I wondered how good his shots might be. I looked forward to comparing our photos, thinking full well that my shots would knock his socks off.

As it turned out, his big buck came right in to less than twenty yards and lingered for several minutes while he got some fantastic shots. Even with his cheapo camera. The fact is, his photos were so darn good, when I saw them after the hunt, it was my socks that needed pulling up.

Dad made a perfect shot when this big buck turned and looked away. (Photo by Eric Pape)

Holy wow. My shots were good, but Dad's shots were great. And his was a different buck than the big one I got. As we looked at each other's cameras and compared shots, I fell to the ground cackling when I saw the awesome photos on his camera.

We got 'em, all right. It was one of our greatest hunts ever. We both got monster bucks, mine being one of the three biggest bucks I'd ever photographed in the wild, and Dad's being the first big buck he ever shot while camera hunting. I gave my hunting partner a hearty handshake of congratulations. Although my buck was a little bigger, I conceded the victory to Dad, who'd clearly won the day with the best quality photos.

While Dad napped, I downloaded his shots to my computer, then went to get some photos printed. When he awoke, I gave him the photos and got a little choked up in the process.

Thinking back over the years, it wasn't too long ago when he was teaching me the ways of the woods and all about hunting. This time it was my turn to be the teacher. In recent years, I'd shared my stories of camera hunting and encouraged him to give it a try. I'd told him of the difficulties and rewards of the game, how to take the shot only when the deer is moving or looking away, and how satisfying it is to get a great shot.

After all the times he'd guided me and brought home photos of my successes, this time it was my turn to be the guide and bring home the pictures of his success. I couldn't have been more proud.

Posing with our trophies after the hunt, it turned out to be one of our best hunts ever.

The old dog learned a new trick and found huge success in the process. Helping him to find that success made it one of the finest moments of my hunting career. I knew right then, whatever might happen the rest of the year, this would be the highlight of my 2018 hunting season.

For what it's worth, my bruiser buck on Saturday morning was a symmetrical four-by-four, about twenty inches wide, with a small ninth point on the right and good mass all around. I'd guess his antlers would measure around 135 inches. Maybe more.

Dad's big buck was a three-by-three, about eighteen inches wide. At first glance, you'd have thought it was a big eight-point, but with a brow-tine missing on its right and a crab-claw fork on the left, it wound up being a whopper six-point.

To complete a spectacular Saturday of hunting, I was able to get some shots in the evening of the same big buck Dad shot that morning. It was a fantastic day as I saw seventeen deer & seven bucks in the morning and twenty-four deer and eight bucks in the evening.

By the time the weekend was over, I'd seen sixty-eight deer and twenty-two bucks in just three days of hunting. It was more deer and many more bucks than I'd see in an entire season in the U.P.

More than anything, it was a great hunt and a memorable adventure with my favorite old hunting partner. As we'd grown older, we'd evolved as hunters. We were still hunting, still sharing the old traditions in our favorite old places, but in new ways we were finding new kinds of hunting success.

After harvesting more than 100 bucks between us, we'd both taken enough bucks in our lives. This time it was more about a father and son sharing life together in the woods, doing what we've always enjoyed. And even though the result didn't include cooked venison, the taste of success was just as sweet. This time it was good enough to simply be there together, to capture the moments and to let the legends live on.

34 EPILOGUE

For me, life went on after the hunt for the Legend. The story played out, and the contents and conclusion of the book unfolded right before my eyes. All I had to do was get it sorted out on paper. It was the journey of a million steps. Now, after a little more than three years, I'm finally wrapping up the loose ends. In a few weeks, we'll finally see this story come to life in the form of a real book. And with the completion of this book, the Legend of Thunder Canyon will achieve a degree of immortality.

Shortly after the conclusion of that incredible 2016 hunt, my story was featured on "Discovering," the local outdoors television show. The two-part show was edited and produced by Brian Whitens of 906 Outdoors. Using actual video I shot during the hunt and additional video he shot after the hunt, Brian did an excellent job of putting the clips together to tell the story. Originally broadcast throughout the Upper Peninsula on the NBC affiliate WLUC-TV, the video can now be purchased on the 906 Outdoors website and can be streamed anytime via YouTube.

The mount of the Legend was completed in early June by taxidermist Mike Anderson of Green Creek Taxidermy in Ishpeming. Delivered as promised and just in time to be seen by our first visitors of the season, the mount was done with great skill and looks fantastic. In the first few days of having the deer on the wall, I did several double-takes, my mind having thought it had seen a real live deer in the living room.

A few months after the season, I had the Legend's antlers measured by the guys at Commemorative Bucks of Michigan. While the final score makes no difference in the value of the experience to me, being a history buff, I wanted to know where the Legend would stand in the history of hunting in Michigan. With an inside spread registering a whopping 23.5 inches and an official net score totaling 131 5/8, the Legend's antlers easily qualified for a place in the all-time record book.

The Legend, at left, and Mr. B. G. on the right. They make all the other bucks look little.

For an eight-pointer, to tally a net score of 131 5/8 is pretty impressive anywhere. But here in the U.P. where winters are always tough, wolves are hungry, and deer populations are near an all-time low, when a deer survives five and a half years and grows to those proportions, he naturally becomes a legend.

According to the CBM big game records, the Legend wound up being the second-largest buck known to be harvested in the U.P. during the 2016 hunting season. Not bad, considering the land area of the U.P. is nearly the size of the states of Vermont and New Hampshire combined. No matter how you look at it, the Legend ended up among elite company.

I'm still not sure where my story ends. As hunters, the stories all roll into one and become the story of our lives. However it goes, it's never over until the end. For now, I look forward to getting back to the woods next season.

When you get to the woods, I wish you well. Be safe, be quiet, and be a good sportsman. Above all, be the best person you can be. They say good things happen to good people. I say good luck comes to good folks. And while it's sometimes better to be lucky than good, it's always best when you can be both lucky and good. So, whenever you can, try to make your own luck.

May the force be with you, and win or lose, on good days and bad, even when it's the farce that's with you, be sure to find a way to have fun. And if you can't do that, at least find a way to make fun of yourself, or your buddy.

Whatever you do, cherish the day, appreciate the company of your partners, savor the scenery, relish the fresh air, and take pleasure in every moment you spend with wildlife in wild places.

In other words, enjoy the hunt.

ABOUT THE AUTHOR

An avid outdoorsman, Duane Pape has been exploring the peninsulas of Michigan for more than forty years. He spent his first twenty-five years in the Lower Peninsula, hiking and hunting in the farmlands of the south and fishing and foraging among the lakes and hills of the north.

In 1996 Duane went further north to explore the mountains and streams of the Upper Peninsula and to study photography at Northern Michigan University. While in school, Duane served as a staff photographer at the Mining Journal and as the photo editor at the North Wind.

Upon the completion of his college education in 2000, Duane served for many years as the athletics photographer at NMU. Having worked as a journalist and photographer for more than twenty years, Duane's photos and writings have appeared in numerous local and regional publications.

Today, Duane resides with his family in a cabin in the woods, somewhere northwest of Marquette. They enjoy listening to the wind, walking in the woods, paddling on the water, catching and releasing beautiful fish, and watching the wonders of the natural world as the seasons unfold.

The author with the catch (and release) of the day.

Made in the USA
Monee, IL
10 October 2023

44329983R00113